Happy birthday to Greg and
alma —
        Wilson
        Aug, 2~,,,,,,

of Haviland *&* Honey

of Haviland & Honey

Myrtle D. Metz

PRUETT

PRUETT PUBLISHING COMPANY
BOULDER, COLORADO

Printed in the United States
10 9 8 7 6 5 4 3 2 1

Library of Congress Cataloging-in-Publication Data

Metz, Myrtle D. (Myrtle Drexel), 1924–
    Of Haviland and honey : a Colorado girlhood, 1924 to 1947 / Myrtle D. Metz.
        p.   cm.
    ISBN 0-87108-814-2 (cloth : acid-free paper)—ISBN 0-87108-825-8 (paper: acid-free paper)
    1. Metz, Myrtle D. (Myrtle Drexel), 1924–   —Childhood and youth.
2. Crawford (Colo.)—Social life and customs. 3. Crawford (Colo.)—
Biography. 4. Depressions—1929—Colorado—Crawford. I. Title.
F784.C793M48   1992
978.8′18—dc20   92-19608
                                                               CIP

Cover and book design by Jody Chapel, Cover to Cover Design, Denver, Colorado
Cover illustration by Kathleen Nichols Lanzoni

Contents

The trifles of our daily lives,
The common things scarce worth recall,
Whereof no visible trace survives,
These are the mainsprings, after all.

—Anonymous

To my daughters, Donna and Linda,
that they may know their heritage.

Acknowledgments

A very special thank-you must go to my husband, Louis—typist, idea man, kindly critic, and long-suffering helper. Without him I simply could not have written anything.

I gratefully acknowledge help from many sources, including *Long Horns and Short Tales: A History of the Crawford Country,* in two volumes, by Mamie Ferrier and George Sibley; Martha Savage, daughter of Crawford's banker; Jean Clark, daughter of Crawford pioneers Agnes and Henry Kraii; Marie Duke, my sister "Rie"; my uncles Raymond and Earl Den Beste; my aunts Leone Den Beste and Edith Etherton; my cousins Dorothy and Dallas Stephens; my friends Arnie Drooz and Gladys Wells; and Dianne Russell, my patient, helpful, and always encouraging editor.

CRAWFORD, COLORADO, IN THE 1930s

Population ~150 ~ Elevation ~ Approx. 6700'

Legend

1. Our home
2. Grandpa Drexel's home
3. Parsonage
4. Church
5. Cemetery
6. Mrs. Coldiron's home
7. Watering station
8. Jail
9. Telephone office
10. Old cheese factory
11. Wilson's store
12. School
13. Flour mill
14. Aunt Grace's home
15. Bank
16. Post office
17. Drugstore
18. Creamery
19. Old hotel
20. Zeldenhuis's store
21. Newspaper office,
    Dance hall,
    Movie theater
22. "Ol' Lewis's store
23. The Van Engens' home
x. Gas stations

Young's Peak

~ Needle Rock
~ Saddle Mountain

Crawford St.

Graham St.

Highway 92

Smith Fork Creek

~ Black Canyon
~ Drexel Ranch
~ Maher
~ Black Mesa

Oak Ave.

School St.

Third St.

Cedar St.

Clipper St.

Cutler Ave.

Clipper Ditch

Scale
Approx. 300'

N

Second St.

Clipper

Highway 92

~ Den Beste's Home

-Delta
-Hotchkiss
-Paonia

 *1. The Trip*

C - O - L - O - R - A - D - O
Tell the world I'm feelin' fine.
'Cause I just got back
To my mile-high shack
In this healthy, wealthy
Wonderful state of mine. . . .

SO GOES an old song I learned when I was a kid. Now it sings itself in my head as the airplane leaves Denver and points west toward the Rockies. Every time I make this trip I am awed again by those massive mountains iced in snow. It takes nearly a day of driving on a modern highway to thread one's way through them but only an hour to fly over them and land on the dry, dusty desert that meets the mountains so abruptly on the western side.

While others more accustomed to this flight than I read or chat with seatmates, I keep my eyes glued on the sights below. I see a crumpled earth in tones of gray, brown, and green, with jagged rocks sticking up at odd angles and ravines etched in the white of last winter's snows. Now, on a June day in the mid 1980s I watch the scene again and hope I won't miss the last ten minutes, when the plane must fly low over Grand Mesa on its way to a landing in Grand Junction.

An aerial view, looking east, of the Crawford country in 1940. The town is in the lower left foreground; Needle Rock is just above and to the left of center. Photograph by Davis Studio, Hotchkiss, Colorado.

This mesa isn't the usual kind of tableland at all, but a range of mountains whose tops were sheared off by a sheet of ice eons ago. What was left was a row of flat tops ten thousand feet high. The airplane must descend from above that monster mesa and immediately find its way to the city, five thousand feet lower. As it passes over the western rim of Grand Mesa, I can pick out deer trails and tall spruce trees and sometimes a toy car or two on the single road that wanders along the scenic edge. I feel like a bird surveying its domain as I look down. And then we drop, and drop, and drop to the brown, flat land where sagebrush and thistles grow, and I know I'm almost home.

Not quite home, though, because first I must ride back up into those mountains—south and east, up and up, past dry gulches and canyons, around hillocks and ridges sculpted by wind and water, until I reach the grassy foothills where the mountains rise from the desert. Finally, there in a little cowtown called Crawford, I really am home.

All these thoughts swirl in my head as the plane rolls to a stop on the airstrip at Grand Junction's terminal and I spot Uncle Howard and Aunt Leone waiting near the gate. Howard is one of my mother's six brothers and the one who looks most like his father, Will Den Beste. Leone is not only my aunt by marriage but also my father's cousin on his mother's side. Such a double relationship is not uncommon in isolated rural communities such as Crawford, but to my city-bred husband it still seems odd.

I step out of the plane and become windblown even before I can reach the gate. It always blows like this, but I forget between trips.

"Oh, it's good to see you! Did you have a good flight? Here, Howard, take Myrtle's coat. Let's go on in and wait for the bags . . . ." I can't get a word in edgewise as Leone continues her nonstop greeting. No matter. I smile to them both and we walk as she rattles on in her pleasant way. Leone is one of those people who talk and laugh to hide feelings of unease or inadequacy, yet she is not inadequate in any way. Strange how we so often misjudge ourselves.

As we load my luggage into the car and start our trip up the valley from Grand Junction, I feel a quickening of my senses. The smell of dust, the clear air that lets one see for miles, the strangeness of the desert landscape—all this I notice with increasing excitement. Then comes the familiar outline of Saddle Mountain and Castle Rock in the distance, the road up through the ranches of Crawford Mesa, and finally Crawford itself.

It's not much of a town, really—just a cluster of modest frame houses surrounding a crossroads where a few businesses have sprouted to meet the demands of this ranching community. In my early childhood there were perhaps three grocery stores, a drugstore, the post office and bank, the schoolhouse and church, three gas stations, and, of course, a pool hall, a saloon, a blacksmith shop, and a hotel. There was even a cheese factory there once. A rather large hall with a stage at one end served at various times as a dance floor, a movie theater, and a place for publishing *The Crawford Chronicle*. Except for the stone school, all these were wooden structures, usually in

The main crossroad in Crawford, about 1940. Notice evidence of horses in the street.

need of paint, with high, square false fronts just like any other frontier town.

And there were boardwalks fronting some of the stores with the usual weeds peeping through the cracks and around the edges. If the boards were wide enough, we could walk on tiptoes chanting, "Step on a crack, you'll break your mother's back . . . Step on a nail, you'll put your dad in jail." If we weren't afraid of lizards and grasshoppers, we could crawl under the highest walks and hunt for money. Pennies were pretty common, nickels were a nifty find, and a dime was a dream come true. Now, in the 1980s, the town seems smaller and a bit drab.

Howard brings me back to the present as he says, "Sorry Louis couldn't come with you. How long can you stay?"

"Lou says he can manage without me for about ten days. I really want to be here long enough to visit everyone."

As I speak we drive past the gray-stone, two-story schoolhouse. It looks deserted—not just vacation-time silent but forlornly empty.

"Didn't you know?" asks Leone. "The Crawford High School was consolidated with the Paonia High School several years ago

The Crawford Community Church in 1990.

and the younger kids are in a new building up above Galyon's place—
you know, above where we used to live."

I can't imagine a building up on that dry hillside of cedars. And
no high school in Crawford? How sad.

As we turn a corner to drive up an unfamiliar street to Howard
and Leone's new house, I see with satisfaction that the white frame
church hasn't changed. There it sits in the middle of town at the
main crossroads, with sprinklers going to keep the lawn on the west
side green. Behind it, the cemetery, also green from faithful watering,
spreads out and up the hillside. In its natural state the land all around
Crawford is a grayish tan, a color I always thought was the normal
color of earth until I lived in South Carolina and found out that
earth can be red sometimes. Now that I've lived in the South for
many years, it is the gray tones that seem strange to me.

As we sit eating our supper of fresh roasting ears, wilted-lettuce
salad, and crisp fried chicken, I gaze out the east window to those
mountains that were such a part of my growing up. There is Saddle
Mountain, so named because when the cone blew out of it in some
ancient eruption, a northern and southern rim with a hollow between

The Crawford Cemetery in 1990. Castle Mountain is in the distance.

was left. Next to it lies the range that forms what is known as Castle Mountain, with a rock formation at its southern end that looks like a castle up near the clouds. And south of that, a valley stretches into the distance, ending in a ridge called Black Mesa; the light strikes that mesa so obliquely that it seems always to be in shadow and appears almost purple, or even black. Or maybe it's called Black Mesa because the soil there is a rich, black loam. These are the mountains that sheltered the first white settlers, that provided homes and food for the Ute Indians before them, and that call me back again and again.

The sky turns to gold, then bronze and red, and finally purple, like the changing colors of an iridescent painting. Darkness comes quickly then, as we sit on the porch and watch lights flicker on in the houses below us. I watch, then listen to the creek farther down the hill as it falls from rock to rock on its way down the Smith Fork Canyon. And I remember my father's words from a long-ago letter: "The creeks are all roaring now, ditches are full, everything is blooming, climate is perfect 20 hours a day and the other four aren't bad. Why would anyone want to be anywhere else?"

The next morning the sun is high and hot in the clear mountain air as I walk down the hill to the middle of Crawford and turn east at the church. If this street coming into town from beyond Saddle Mountain has a name, I've forgotten it. Not that it matters. Everyone knows everyone else and needs no directions for getting around.

The paths and yards all seem as familiar as old shoes. The two Drexel houses stand less than two hundred yards or so beyond the church, and in no time at all I am there, hardly knowing which direction to look first, scarcely daring to look at all.

The house I grew up in still stands below the street, on the south side. There have been many changes, but it is recognizable and, most importantly, it still looks neat and lived-in. A well-clipped lawn, healthy trees, a new garage—all attest that the young man who bought this house from Daddy in the 1950s has loved and cared for it through the intervening years.

Across the street on the uphill side stands Grandpa's and Grandma's house. I turn to look at it and feel a sense of dismay. Can it possibly be this bad? I know it hasn't been lived in for the past few months, but how can it look so run-down? What would the folks think if they could come back to life and see it now?

I can imagine each individual reaction. Grandpa, a tight-lipped frown on his face, would sit down on the nearest step, take out the pen and paper that always seemed to be conveniently hidden in a vest pocket, and start to draw up a Plan of Renewal in his precise, neat handwriting. Grandma, all six feet of her angular frame quivering with rage, would grab the nearest hoe and start chopping out the offending weeds, daring them ever to show their heads again. Momma would wring her hands and cry out in anguish, "Oh, how awful! Oh, Clarence, how can I bear it? Oh, dear, oh dear!" Daddy would say, "Now, Esther, everything will be all right. Just have a little patience." And he would quietly gather up the tools needed to make repairs and set to work. And in no time at all (in my imagination) the Drexel home would be restored to its former beauty. It would again be a substantial two-story house with a wide porch and magnificent leaded windows; manicured green lawns; borders of roses, peonies, lilies, and columbine; stately trees of all kinds; and a vegetable garden laid out in orderly rows in the gully west of the house, like a Grandma Moses painting.

My Drexel grandparents' home in Crawford in its heyday. Young's Peak is behind.

I turn to look back up the street toward town. How dusty that street always used to be before the days of oiling and paving! The gravel the county sometimes spread on it would help keep mud under control in the winter months, but it did nothing for the summer dust. Every time a car or wagon went by, it was accompanied by the *crunch crunch* of wheels on the gravel and clouds of dust pluming behind, like smoke.

I walk back slowly, enjoying the hot sun on my head and the odor of roses climbing the fence near the Parsonage. The house is no longer a parsonage, but it hasn't changed much. It still seems to lean a little to the east. When I was small I supposed that was because heaven was somewhere east of the mountains.

Across the street from the Parsonage, where several new prefab homes now sit, looking like city cousins slightly uncomfortable in their new country environment, there used to be a sod hut with a dirt floor and windows made of pieces of glass salvaged from some dump. Mrs. Coldiron lived there, a woman of uncertain age and the most vigorous laugh I've ever heard. You could hear her all the way to town. It was a good laugh, though, and I don't ever remember hearing anyone complain about it, although it could wake you from a sound afternoon nap. I used to wonder why she didn't live in a regular house like ours and why she was so poor.

Next to Mrs. Coldiron's place there was a water station. It was a big wooden tank on stilts that was filled with water from a pipe connected to the town-owned spring, located some miles away on the slope of Land's End Mountain. There was a spigot near the bottom of the tank. Ranchers and farmers came to fill barrels with drinking and cooking water there, paying by the barrel. Since the hitching rail was conveniently located beside the water station, there would often be several wagons with their teams hitched along the rail, the horses patiently waiting for the men to finish a drink down at the saloon and impatiently flicking away flies with their tails.

But what did people do for water back in the very early days, I wonder? What was life like for those early settlers? Why didn't I ask these questions when I was young and my family was there to answer them? Youth is so blissfully ignorant! Now I must find what answers I can. And my thoughts turn to Grandpa Drexel and what it must have been like when he first came to the Crawford country.

2. The Pioneer from Maryland

GRANDPA DREXEL headed west from Baltimore in 1892. I found out about it one Saturday quite by accident when I was spending the gloomy November afternoon looking at his scrapbook. Sitting on the window seat in Grandma's dining room and idly turning the yellowed pages of the thick book, I noticed something very odd on one page. It looked like bark, but it was white, like paper.

"What is it, Grandpa? Where did you get it?"

"That's birch bark, my dear." He was quiet for a moment, musing; then his eyes gleamed as he continued: "And thereby hangs a tale." Grandpa's voice took on a meditative tone as he told me about the day he picked up this piece of birch bark in the woods near the sanitorium where he was staying. It was in the Adirondacks, and he had gone there hoping the tuberculosis that was sapping his strength might be conquered in the clear mountain air, away from the fog and grime of Baltimore.

The son of a fairly prosperous perfume-maker, Frank Drexel had been raised in a strict German home and educated in a nearby Lutheran school. He was well educated for his day, knew the classics well, and loved to go to the theater and the opera. He had accepted this temporary exile to the mountains with good grace; but now the doctors had told him that he seemed to be getting worse rather than better. Perhaps—well, they had said, there was one possible course of action. He could go to the western lands where the air was much cleaner and drier. Some people seemed to benefit from this change and, really, there wasn't anything else to suggest.

The West! Thousands of miles from his beloved home and all the civilized pursuits of life? What would he do with himself there? And, if he did get better, what could he do to make a living? From the little he had read about this huge, sparsely settled part of the country, he envisioned it as a wild, untamed wilderness where cowboys lived on horseback, Indians fought the white settlers, and people knew nothing about the niceties of life.

But of course that couldn't be entirely true. After all, there was Denver with its Brown Palace Hotel and its new, elegant, gold-domed capitol building. There were stories about them in the *Baltimore Sun.* And there was the opera house at Central City, where musicians from the East performed every year. Some of his favorite opera stars had sung there, he told me.

Well, he had decided, no use worrying about it: If that's where he had to go to survive, he'd go. Opportunities come to those who take action—that was his motto. He began to study every article in the *Sun* that might illuminate that remote country for him. And he wrote to a friend who had already gone west. The answering letter was a deciding factor. Yes, this new country *was* the land of opportunity, his friend wrote. There was a lot of homestead land just for the asking.

And so it was that, at the age of twenty-four, my grandfather left his family and friends and set his course for a spot west of Denver, where his friend said many people were finding land. He took with him his most cherished possessions: several leather-bound volumes of Shakespeare and other classics, his German Bible, and a few scores of favorite operas, including some of the new Gilbert and Sullivan operettas that were such hits in the East. He even packed his spats and top hat, hoping to use them in Denver sometime.

A more unlikely looking pioneer probably could not have been found anywhere. Frank Drexel stood only five feet seven inches tall and was pale and sickly, obviously unused to "roughing it." He had dark, short, just slightly wavy hair, pale but alert blue eyes, a long pointed nose that rather resembled a beak, and a straight, thin-lipped mouth that didn't smile easily.

The Crawford stage on its way to Maher in the early 1900s.

He never told me, nor have I found a record of his impressions of that trip west or of his opinion of Denver when he got there. How he traveled from Denver to the Western Slope can only be surmised. There was a train going south from Denver to Colorado Springs, and from there through canyons and passes to the western side of the Rockies. By 1893, the railroad had made its way to a rather settled community called Hotchkiss at the base of the foothills of the Smith Fork Valley. At that point, transportation became more rugged.

A stage met the train three or four times a week to transport supplies to the settlers in the Smith Fork Valley and to deliver mail to the little post offices at Crawford and Maher, even farther up in the hills. The distance from Hotchkiss to Crawford is eleven miles on today's paved road, but that early road would have been longer and slower. Little more than a trail smoothed clear of rocks and brush through the heavy clay soil, it wound through the hills and around fenced property. It would have taken half a day to go from Hotchkiss all the way to Maher. The stage was nothing more than a horse-drawn wagon, but it was the lifeblood of all the people trying to make new lives in those hills and valleys. Passengers were welcome to share the ride, of course, so it's quite probable that young

Frank Drexel's first home in Colorado.

Frank's first glimpse of his new home was from the jump seat of the Crawford Stage.

I don't know how Grandpa Drexel found a place to live or why he chose beekeeping as a way to earn a livelihood. I only know that he did and that his first home was a long, low structure with a sod roof somewhere up near Maher. Maps of Colorado show Maher as a town just like Crawford, but it never has been anything but a post office and a schoolhouse. It was named for one of my ancestors, a great-grandfather who had made his way to the Colorado mountains in the 1880s and homesteaded in the high valley below Black Mesa. Those first settlers came on horseback or on foot from the east through Gunnison and over Black Mesa by using an old Ute Indian trail. Great-Grandpa Caleb Maher found it very hard to live in isolation without regular mail service and decided to try to get a post office in his home. He walked back east to Gunnison, seventy miles away across the mountains, to make the application to the government. When asked what the name of the post office should be, he said he didn't care just as long as he got one. The only name that came to his mind was his own; that's how the town of Maher got its name.

One of Caleb Maher's children was a girl named Ella. Sometime during the fall of 1895, she and Frank Drexel met at a Literary

Society meeting. It would be hard to imagine two people more unlike. Ella Maher was tall and gawky, strong-willed and impetuous, with the spirit of an untamed filly. Manners, grace, and composure would come to her later, after many years of effort. But she had a tremendous thirst for knowledge and a love of literature. The Literary Society was just the place for two such people as Frank and Ella to learn to know each other.

They were married in 1897, and Caleb deeded a corner of his land to them as a wedding present. The house they built was patterned after the two-story dwellings of the Maryland countryside. It had a big kitchen and pantry, a dining room, a parlor, and a bedroom all on the first floor, and another bedroom upstairs. Under the house was a dirt cellar for storing food and a rock-lined cistern that held a year's supply of domestic water. The cistern was filled in the early spring from a nearby creek during the first snowmelt days, when the water would be pure and clean. There was a wide porch, shaded by woodbine and morning glory vines, wrapped around two sides of the house. A carefully tended climbing rose framed the entrance to the outhouse near the back door. And in the front, a fine lawn and a row of tall poplar trees completed the small estate. It was called The Ranch, and its crop was honey, rather than cattle, sheep, or alfalfa.

Frank and Ella wasted no time in starting a family, and within a little more than two years they had two sons: Frank Jr. and Clarence. Frank, the older of the two, grew to be a handsome and very bright boy, but he inherited his mother's impetuous temper, which he often inflicted on his younger brother. Poor little Clarence was not only younger but was also rather sickly and not well equipped to fight back. The two boys grew up not exactly disliking each other, but less than close.

They certainly were not spoiled. They walked two and a half miles both to and from school, and after arriving home had a number of chores to do. Up until the acquisition of the family's Model T Ford, they rode horseback or hitched up their wagon to ride the three miles to Crawford. As the boys grew older they learned the beekeeping business and eventually became partners with their father.

Raising bees is a common enough pursuit among weekend farmers—a hive or two, a dozen combs of delicious honey, the fun

The Ranch in its glory days, around 1928.

of watching those interesting insects in their communal activities—all this frequently becomes a hobby for many suburbanites. But producing enough honey to earn a comfortable income is another matter altogether. By the time Frank and Ella had raised their two sons and those boys in turn had started families of their own, The Ranch included twelve bee yards with twenty-five to thirty hives in each yard, a storage shed for supplies, a garage with a workshop at one end, and a "honey house," or extracting room.

To my sisters and me, the honey house was a place of fascination and fear. There we had to walk past an eight-foot-tall furnace that produced steam to run all the machinery for extracting honey and melting down beeswax. Everything hissed and roared and clanged and emitted heat. And everything was sticky. But worst of all, there were bees in there. No matter that Daddy assured us over and over that as long as we left the bees alone they would pay no attention to us; never mind that Grandpa said the bees were after honey, not little girls—it still took all the courage we could muster to walk past that inferno of a furnace and into the big room where bees constantly buzzed overhead. But it was worth it. Uncle Frank and Daddy stood at a sort of table where they cut off the

A bee yard behind the honey house and sheds at The Ranch.

beeswax cappings from the combs with steam knives. As those cappings curled away from the hot knife with honey glistening all over them, the men would pick off a portion of the gooey mess and deposit it in any outstretched hands. Nothing I've ever tasted quite equals the exquisite flavor of hot honey and beeswax.

Across the room were two huge tubs with brackets all around the inside edges for holding the decapped frames of honey. When the tubs were switched on they literally whirled the honey out of the combs. We could see it as it turned the inside of the tubs to a shimmering gold. From the tubs, the honey flowed into a vat about six feet tall, where it settled until all the impurities and bits of wax had risen in a foamy crust to the top. Clear, pale yellow honey was then piped from the bottom of the vat into waiting honey cans, each capable of holding sixty pounds of honey, and after those cans were filled they were loaded into the honey truck and taken to the storage shed.

Some years Grandpa and his two sons produced and sold as much as two railroad cars full of honey. That's sixty thousand pounds—a lot of honey! But the income from that crop had to supply the needs of three families. If a fellow liked working with bees—and my father did—it provided a satisfying way to make a modest living.

Uncle Frank had no fear of bees, but he didn't like them or the job of beekeeping. He was stuck in the rut of working at a distasteful job simply because he had a young family to support.

"I think I'll move to Hotchkiss and get a bookkeeping job," he'd say at the end of a hot, sticky day in the extracting room. "No mess, no stings, no heavy lifting—now that's what I'd call a good job."

"You sure you'd want to give up being part of Frank H. Drexel and Sons?" Grandpa kept his voice reasonable, but the spark in his blue eyes and his drawn brows would betray the annoyance this conversation always aroused in him.

"Hell, this is just plain peasant work!"

"Well, it's always your choice, of course—you know that. But don't forget you have a lot of free time during the winter with bee work."

"Yeah, and I'm going to use some of that free time to start looking for something else to do—a businessman's job for a change." And Uncle Frank's handsome face would flush with anger as he tossed wax-encrusted supers* into the truck.

My father usually found a way to absent himself discreetly during such discussions. He had learned through long experience that his older brother's anger often vented itself on him. What's more, he honestly didn't understand Frank's aversion to beekeeping. But Frank had always rebelled, as if it were part of his nature to do so, while Clarence had always been accepting and obedient.

In fact, the two brothers were different in many ways. Both had been away from The Ranch for their education, first to the county seat of Delta for their high-school training, and then to the Agricultural College at Fort Collins. Clarence liked the academic life and graduated with a degree in forestry. Frank, on the other hand, felt restless and trapped in school. After two years of college he had gone back home with no real goal for his future and had let himself get caught in his father's business. He hadn't been happy since.

Now each of the brothers had a family, a house to pay for, and a part-interest in the family business. It was more than many of their neighbors had, and not something to toss away lightly.

One problem for Frank was that his wife, Grace, was overly ambitious for her family. She had grown up in Denver and was used to the many activities available to a city youngster. It was her

---

*A super is the removable upper story of a beehive.

From left: *Clarence and Frank (Jr.) Drexel as young men.*

firm belief that any decently educated child should have music, dancing, and elocution lessons and should learn as many social skills and arts as possible. Most of these things were out of reach in our mountain town, but she provided what she could. There were children's magazines, books, dolls, and toys, plus a first-class gym set with swings, seesaw, rings, and monkey bar at her home.

Mary Edith, Frank's and Grace's first child, was precocious and charming and dominated everyone around her. She would probably become an actress, everyone thought. The next child, Frank Ralph, made it plain from the beginning that he wasn't intimidated by his big sister or anything else. He wasn't mean, just totally fearless. And then there was baby Dorothy—a tiny, quiet image of her mother. Because Aunt Grace was a very small person herself, you would be accurate in thinking of Dorothy as a little doll. She was a contented little girl, and never tried to compete with Mary Edith or Ralph.

All the Drexel children spent happy hours playing at Aunt

The scene of the burned-down Ranch in 1932. Grandma and Grandpa Drexel are sitting in front of the honey house.

Grace's house. It wasn't far for us to walk, even though it was clear across town. We loved Aunt Grace, the toys, and all the rest of it. Besides that, two ditches ran through the front yard, and we were allowed to play in them whenever the water was low.

But when I was eight, something happened that altered all our lives. It was deep wintertime, and all the fields and roads were smothered in snow. We had just eaten our Saturday breakfast when the phone rang. Daddy answered it while Momma started to clear dishes from the table. When he turned away from the phone everything stopped dead. His face was ashen. "The Ranch is on fire! Fix me some sandwiches, Ma, while I get the truck started. Central is calling everybody and I'll pick up a bunch of fellas at the drugstore as soon as I can get going."

He hurried out to the back porch for his high-topped overshoes, collected an ax and shovel, started the truck, and in five minutes came back in to pick up the sandwiches and give Momma a kiss.

For hours and hours we heard nothing. All I could think of was The Ranch covered in flames. Were Grandma and Grandpa all right? Would everything burn up and we'd never again hear our favorite record, "The Bell Song" from the opera *Lakmé,* on the

Victrola? And the stereopticon and all those wonderful slides of the Grand Canyon and the Cascades—would they burn up? And what about the pump organ Grandma loved to play?

The house did burn—right to the ground, leaving a gaping, blackened hole where the cellar and cistern had been. It was a devastating sight. But the workshop, garage, honey house, and storage shed were all saved. And because the house burned slowly, the men were able to save nearly all its contents, even such things as the Christmas tree ornaments brought from Germany many years ago. I have never been able to understand how they did that, because the fire started in the chimney near the roof, and those ornaments were stored in the attic.

Grandma and Grandpa put most of their possessions in the storage shed and moved the essential things into the shop, where there was a small coal stove. By the time they had lived in that room for a year, it seemed quite natural to think of the shed as the house where Grandma lived.

One piece of furniture that didn't get stored was the Victrola. Grandpa brought it down to our house in Crawford, "For the duration," he said. I didn't know what a duration was, but I fervently hoped it meant forever. We already had a piano that I was trying hard to learn to play, but the music the record player produced was a revelation in sound and certainly beat what I could do on the piano.

The phonograph used two kinds of needles—steel and wood. Each had an advantage: The steel needle lasted for at least a dozen records while the wooden one had to be sharpened or replaced after each record, but it sounded more mellow. Whenever I was allowed to play a record I chose the wooden needle, not only because it sounded better but because I liked to sharpen it. I would lay it in a little box where a device like a tiny guillotine sliced off the used edge and made a new point. I liked to wind the Victrola too, not tight enough to break the spring, but enough so it wouldn't run down before the record ended. Now, as I listen to my modern stereo with its dual speakers, its tweeters and woofers, its fine balancing gadgets, I marvel at how much we all gloried in the music that came from that primitive machine.

What, I wondered, were Grandpa's thoughts as he listened to

that same music? Perhaps he remembered happy days in Baltimore, grand opera houses and concert halls, glorious voices, and tumultuous ovations. He gave no indication of his thoughts, but sat quietly in rapt attention, elbows on the chair arms and fingertips pressed together, while a little smile played round his mouth.

3. The Pioneers from Iowa

WILL AND Nettie Den Beste, my mother's parents, emigrated from Iowa to Colorado in 1906. They were part of a large group of Dutch people who were lured to the Crawford country by a project named the "Fruitland Land, Water and Livestock Company." The idea was to construct a reservoir in the high mountain valley south of Crawford, then to build ditches from it to a large arid mesa just south of town. Fruitland Mesa had no water and so had never been cultivated, but it was presumed to be fertile. It was looked upon as a bonanza to farmers and ranchers looking for land of their own.

This fantastic proposal was conceived by a man named Willard Gould and his two sons, and the whole thing became known as the "Gould Reservoir Project." It cost more than two hundred thousand dollars and wasn't completed until 1910.

Nettie Den Beste's father, John Sipma, accepted the job of foreman for the building of the reservoir. He persuaded his whole family—his sons, his daughters, and their families—to go with him. None of the women really wanted to leave Iowa, but they had no say in the matter.

The Den Bestes had two little girls then, Esther and Kate. My mother, Esther, the older of the two, told me once she could remember the trip west a little bit—the dirty, noisy train; the strange look

My maternal grandparents, William and Nettie Den Beste, in 1936.

of mountains rising like clouds along the western horizon; and finally a long, tiring, frightening ride in a wagon.

"Was it a covered wagon?" I asked, entranced at the idea that my mother might have been one of those famous pioneers.

"I don't remember whether it was covered or not—it was just a rough wagon. We started out from Sapinero on a dirt road that went up and up and became a sort of trail. I was afraid all the way."

"What were you afraid of?" She had never mentioned any of this before, and I was fascinated.

"Well, I don't know really. It was all so strange—roaring creeks, strange animals, mountains all around us. And the wagon kept tilting as though it might fall over any minute. The trail was full of ruts and rocks and muddy spots. I still wonder how we made it."

Although Grandpa Drexel had traveled by train from Denver on to Delta and Hotchkiss and had thus approached Crawford from the west, most of the early settlers used the southern route that wound up over Black Mesa from Gunnison and Sapinero—a more direct way, but hardly easier. There were stories of people having to tie ropes from the wagons to the saddle horns of mounted riders who were on the uphill side of the trail in order to keep the wagons from tipping over. This route was so steep that it sometimes took three teams of horses to drag a wagon load to the top. Coming down on the Crawford side was just as hard. Some folks tied logs to the back of the wagons to act as drags. The trip took nerve and probably no small measure of desperation.

John Sipma and his party found land on Fruitland Mesa near other Dutch settlers. Their first summer was spent choosing land, clearing ground for gardens, and building cabins. The earth was rocky and dusty, nothing like Iowa's soft, rich soil. The water would change that, or so everyone hoped. Evidence of Indians was everywhere. Children of the new settlers picked up bucketfuls of arrowheads and played with them. Deer and jackrabbits abounded, and although they provided welcome meat, they also trampled and ate the new gardens. At night the coyotes howled and whined in chorus and mountain lions screamed with a peculiarly human cry, enough to make the stoutest heart cringe.

Nettie, used to neatness, cleanliness, and a nice house, found this life very trying. She was homesick and overworked. No matter how much she scrubbed and cleaned the little three-room cabin, the constant wind brought in dust. All the water had to be hauled in from a creek and boiled. She toiled as she had never done before and seemed to have nothing to show for it. But she was essentially a healthy young woman—blonde, sturdy, gray-eyed, and round-faced. She and Will began to acquire a rapidly growing family—three more girls and then a string of six boys.

Their fortune, however, did not grow as fast as their family. In fact, it didn't take many summers before they realized they would never make a fortune on Fruitland Mesa. They had settled on the west end of the mesa where most of the Dutch families had formed a community, but the new Gould Reservoir often didn't supply enough water to reach that end of Fruitland Mesa, especially in late summer. They had planted their land in orchards, but orchards, it turned out, didn't do well there. The growing season was too short at this high elevation to produce a good crop. They persevered but did not prosper.

In spite of trouble and disappointment, the Den Bestes were always sustained by their strong Dutch Reform faith and their close family ties. And they never lost sight of their belief in two other fundamentals: cleanliness and the need for education. One could be dirt poor but never dirty. One could be without money, but to be mentally lazy was out of the question.

Nettie had gotten a high school education and gone to the Northwestern Classical Academy in Iowa. She wasted no time in starting classes for her children and the neighbor's youngsters. Will had the more usual eighth grade education but had gotten some musical training along the way. He taught all his children to read music, play an instrument, and sing.

Esther found the world of books and learning so rewarding that she made up her mind to continue school after eighth grade, even though she would have to leave home to do it. She found a place in Hotchkiss where she could work for room and board, and her folks agreed to pay the high-school tuition.

This was the nearest high school, about ten miles away from the Mesa. But what a treacherous ten miles it was—down the steep, narrow, twisting Anderson Grade, across the creek on a narrow wooden bridge, up the other side of Smith Fork Canyon, and then across the windblown fields and wasteland into Hotchkiss. The wagon trip home on Saturday often took the horses a couple of hours, and my mother told me that one winter weekend they got lost in a blizzard and didn't get home until after midnight.

"How did you meet Daddy, if you went to school in Hotchkiss and he went to school in Delta?" I asked her one time. She laughed her sometimes happy, silvery laugh as she recalled those earlier days. "Oh, I didn't meet Clarence until after I graduated from high school. I was working in Sweet's store when I met your father."

"Where was Sweet's store?"

"In Crawford. You know, the place next to the telephone office. I was trying to save money to go to Fort Collins. I wanted to get a degree in home economics."

"Did you? Did you go to college?"

"Well, I went for one year. But I had to earn my room, board, books, tuition—everything. It was hard . . ."

One year was all she got. But she had set the standard for the whole family and nearly all the rest managed to go to college too.

About the time Esther left home to go to Fort Collins, the Den Bestes finally gave up the effort to save their Fruitland Mesa place. They moved to a rented fruit ranch west of Crawford on the rim of the Smith Fork Canyon. The orchards there were well watered by the Clipper Ditch and the land was low enough in elevation to ensure decent crops. It was this second home that I knew as "Gramma Den Beste's" house.

Gramma's sister Jennie and Jennie's husband, Ed Te Grotenhuis, also moved from Fruitland. They settled on Rogers Mesa, west of Hotchkiss. One brother left Colorado to become a railroad employee. The two youngest brothers eventually went back to Iowa, I think. Only the old folks, John Sipma and his wife, stayed on Fruitland Mesa to the end. I can remember visiting them there once or twice.

Even in the "new" house life remained hard for the large Den Beste family. Altogether there were eleven children, and all but one lived to maturity. You would think a family of that size would require a large house, but their new home couldn't, by any stretch of the imagination, be called big or even roomy. It was a log house with rough wooden flooring that was covered with linoleum. There was a medium-sized room, a smaller parlor, and two tiny bedrooms in the main structure. The kitchen seemed to be an afterthought, tacked on like a shed beside the main room. And across the road was a cabin called the "bunkhouse," where all the boys slept. Since no plumbing had been connected to this farm, water had to be hauled in. Ditch water was kept in barrels to be used for washing clothes and dishes. For drinking, cooking, and bath water, Grampa went to the town's water tank. He filled three ten-gallon milk cans (five cents each) and carted them home between the front and back seats of the old "Chevy." Gramma saved rainwater and melted clean snow during the winter months. This most precious fluid was carefully meted out—so much for cooking, so much for dish-washing, and so much for bathing. They did not waste water in that household. In fact, they didn't waste anything. Cloth scraps became quilts and old stockings became rugs. Buttons, yarn, old shoes—all were saved to patch other things. Food scraps got saved, along with the water drained from cooked vegetables, to slop the pigs. Catalogues went to the privy to be used as toilet paper.

Earl was the baby in the Den Beste family, the last of the six boys. He was born just three months before I was—my uncle but my playmate from the very first. So his Mama was my Gramma.

The Den Beste farm and fruit ranch on the Smith Fork Canyon in 1930. The garden is in the foreground and an edge of the orchard appears at left. The road separates the main house, on the right, from the "bunkhouse."

I loved to go down to Gramma Den Beste's house and spend the day. We fed the chickens or rolled barrel hoops up and down the hills, romped in the barn where the doves cooed constantly and hay smelled dusty and dry, or played marbles behind the bunkhouse. We made up a fine marble game with holes that was something like miniature golf. And we played hide-and-seek all over the place: root cellar, outhouse, bunkhouse, or down in the hollow between the house and barn.

If Grampa would let us, sometimes we "helped" at the packing shed in the orchard. It could be fun to sort apples where they were spread out on the sorting table. The only trouble was that the older boys would often tease me—Lester especially. He was next in age before Earl. "Here's Myrtle, the turtle, in a big fat girdle." Or "How's dirty Myrt?" I hated teasing but didn't dare show it around the Den Bestes. Teasing could have been their middle name.

At noon we took turns washing our hands in the enamel basin behind the kitchen door. Then we sat down at the long dining table on various odd chairs. Apple boxes were brought in to help with seating when company came.

First, we bowed our heads for silent grace, then Grampa read a chapter from the Bible. He had been doing this from the first days of his marriage, I think. In fact, he probably had heard the Good Book read aloud all his life. I've heard that he knew it in Dutch as a child, but by the time I came along, the family Bible was the King James version. When he got to the end of Revelation he started over again with Genesis. Sometimes it was boring, especially the part with the "begats." But I liked the story about Esther and was glad they had named Momma for that beautiful queen.

The best time to visit the Den Beste grandparents was on Sunday afternoon. Sunday was special, a day for Sunday school and church, for fried chicken and chocolate cake, and for a family gathering in the afternoon. There would be all of the older children with their families and all the boys who were still at home. When all the Den Beste children were present, there would be Momma, Kate, Ethel, and Edith, with their families, and the six boys: Jim, Howard, Walter, Raymond, Lester, and Earl. We would visit on the porch and lawn, play croquet or "pass-and-touch," or stay inside and play anagrams. Then we'd gather near the piano and sing. Everyone in that family could sing. Grampa sang bass, the boys all knew how to divide up on the men's parts, Gramma sang a clear, lovely melody, and the girls took their pick of alto or soprano. After we had sung a few hymns, the men would do some male quartets and then the women would take their turns with duets and trios. The last song was always "The Awakening Chorus," not only because it was a fitting climax but because voices usually gave out after the effort required to perform that rousing anthem.

Most of the time Gramma seemed tired or sad, or maybe both. But when we sang, her face lit up with a special glow. She was rather pretty, or would have been if she hadn't had to work so hard. She was plump by the time I knew her, and her blonde, softly waved hair was pulled back in a bun. She loved children and made all of us feel very special.

Grampa was harder to understand. He seemed happiest when he was singing, listening to ball games on the radio, or playing checkers or five-hundred. I think that life to him had become grim

Four generations of my family. Clockwise from upper left: *Nettie and William Den Beste, my maternal grandparents; Ella and Frank Drexel, my paternal grandparents; Esther and Clarence Drexel, my parents; Caleb Maher, my great-grandfather, who is holding me; Ardena and John Sipma, my great-grandparents.*

and full of trouble, and he found little joy in any of it except when he could lose himself in one of those pastimes with his family. I seldom saw the happy twinkle in his eyes that often lurked behind Grandpa Drexel's smile. But, on the other hand, I never heard Grandpa Drexel sing with marvelous abandon—in fact, he could hardly sing at all.

4. 1930–1933

I WAS in the first grade and I was in trouble. Not with the teacher, Mrs. Gingrich, whom I adored, and not with schoolwork or grades, because school was easy. But something seemed to be making me sick all the time. Every few weeks I would develop a fever, a sore throat, and an earache. Momma and Daddy tried every remedy they knew: a drink of hot honey and lemonade, warm woolen cloths soaked in camphor and laid on my chest or back, smelly hot Musterole rubbed on my skin, sweet oil in my ears, Jello and chicken broth. All of it was useless.

Finally Daddy called Dr. Haley, who lived in Paonia, fifteen miles away. Fifteen miles by the good roads, that is. Dr. Haley, however, took the most direct route. If there was a cow path or trail of any kind, he took it. His ability to cross the muddy "dobies," an area of treacherous clay soil, was legendary. He was really typical of country doctors of that time: delivering babies, taking out appendixes and tonsils, lancing boils and carbuncles, and tending to various illnesses throughout half the county.

When Dr. Haley arrived, he looked me over from top to bottom, then talked quietly to Momma and Daddy in the living room. The long, low-voiced conference told my frightened, fevered brain that either I was going to die or be an invalid the rest of my life. As it turned out, what they decided was that I would have to be taken to Grand Junction, ninety miles away, where a specialist would decide if I was strong enough to have my tonsils and adenoids removed. It all sounded so ominous that I decided I'd really rather die.

But when I heard that Grandma Drexel would be the one to take me, I changed my mind. Grandma made things fun, especially when she could go somewhere, and most especially when she did the driving. A trip was always an adventure when Grandma was at the wheel.

The "Jitney," the three Drexel families' Model A Ford, was loaded with blankets and hot-water bottles to keep us warm, and we started off early in the morning. At first it was fun because Grandma drove faster than Daddy did and made games of counting telephone poles. But soon it just seemed like a long ride, and my ears began to ache and I began to feel tired and scared.

The specialist was very nice and very sure the operation should be performed right away the next morning. I remember being put to sleep with ether and waking up with an incredibly sore throat and wondering if the operation had been a failure. And I remember being at someone's house for days and days while Grandma, and everyone else, tried to get me to swallow something. We finally settled on ice cream. It seemed to slip down with less pain than anything else did.

It took two weeks to get me strong enough to make the trip home. I must have been very weak, because I have no memory of that trip or of the homecoming—only of many hours spent near the space heater with books, puzzles, crayons, and paper dolls. Momma made all kinds of special foods, as she said, "to help me get my strength back." Daddy sometimes bundled me up in heavy wraps, took me out to the barn with him, and let me watch him milk Suzy. There was a kind of warm satisfaction in watching milk squirt into the pail between Daddy's legs while Suzy made soft grunting sounds in her throat. The kitty came too, and rubbed against every available leg, tail aquiver, waiting for the warm foam that would soon be poured into her bowl from the top of the pail. Several times I tried to milk the cow under Daddy's direction, but I could never get the hang of it.

There is a curious gap in my memory about this time. And my younger sister, Ellen Marie—"Rie"—doesn't know about it either because she was barely three at the time. It's a fact that my sister Katy was born that year, but I can't remember it. I also know that although Katy was born healthy, Momma seemed to be sick for a long time after the birth. Little snatches and snippets of barely recalled things float back through my memory—Momma crying "I feel like I'm dying!" and Daddy saying, ever so gently, "Now, now, Honey, just hold my hand and you'll feel better in a minute"; Grandma Drexel taking little Rie for a ride in the Jitney; Gramma Den Beste rocking baby Katy in our small wooden rocking chair and urging Momma to "go get a cup of cocoa to calm your nerves."

Of course, I didn't know then about Billy. He came just a year and a half after I did. But he was born with a faulty stomach valve. A big-city doctor might have saved the baby boy, but our country doctor could offer no real help. Billy simply starved to death while my parents stood by helplessly, watching the tiny infant struggle and fail.

That tragedy, and two more babies so soon afterward, was too much to cope with, and Momma became ill for months with what is now known to be depression.

All this, as I say, I learned much later. My actual remembrances are pretty vague. What I do recall clearly was a shift in sleeping arrangements. Katy got too big for her basket and had to be moved into the crib. That meant that Rie, now three, had to leave the crib and join me in the double bed in the front bedroom. Neither of us liked the change very much, and we squabbled every night.

"You're on my side!"

"No I'm not! Get your foot back on your side."

Finally Daddy put a stop to all the fuss by rolling up an old sheet lengthwise and laying it down the middle of the bed between us.

"Now kids, I don't want to hear another word out of you. Go to sleep." The sheet stayed there for a week or so while we got used to each other, then it quietly disappeared.

Both of us now look back on that time as being rather special. Nearly every night Momma would read a story and sing a song to "help us get sleepy." Her favorite song was Eugene Field's poem, "The Little Tin Soldier," set to music by Ethelbert Nevin.

> The little toy dog is covered with dust
> But sturdy and staunch he stands;
> And the little toy soldier is red with rust

And the musket it molds in his hands.
Time was when the little toy dog was new,
And the soldier was passing fair;
And that was the time when our Little Boy Blue
Kissed them and put them there.

"Now, don't you go 'til I come," he said,
"And don't you make any noise!"
So, toddling off to his trundle-bed,
He dreamt of his pretty toys;
And, as he was dreaming, an angel song
Awakened our Little Boy Blue—
Oh! the years are many, the years are long,
But the little toy friends are true!

Aye, faithful to Little Boy Blue they stand,
Each in the same old place,
Awaiting the touch of a little hand,
And the smile of a little face;
And they wonder, as waiting the long years thro'
In the dust of that little chair,
Oh what has become of our Little Boy Blue,
Since he kissed them and put them there.

By the end of that sad tale Rie would be sobbing in the pillow.
But through her tears she always pleaded "Sing it again, Momma,
please, sing it again."

While Momma sang about her sorrow, Daddy put his grief to
work building his three little girls a playhouse. Using lumber from
the burned-out ranch, he created a miniature residence for us. It
had a front porch with a trellis for a rose bush and a tiny attic over
the front porch with a ladder to it. Two little girls could hide up
there and tell secrets all afternoon. The back door opened on to
a little stoop and a backyard with its own sand pile and swing. Inside
there was room for two or three children, the doll's crib, a table
and two chairs, and a kitchen cabinet stocked with cooking utensils
and tin dinnerware. Momma made a tablecloth and a small rug for
the floor and pretty curtains for the windows. The playhouse became
our summer residence. We cooked and cleaned and rocked our dolls
and even slept there on occasion.

All our cousins played there with us, especially Aunt Kate and

My sister Rie on her tricycle, called in those days a "Kiddy Kar."

Uncle Bill Van Engen's children. Their oldest was Wilma Jean, whom we called Jeanie. She was Rie's age, had red hair, a beautiful singing voice, and was hampered physically by crutches and leg braces made necessary by a bout with polio. Young people today don't know the fear polio, often called "infantile paralysis," held for us in those days. Every community was hit by the disease sooner or later.

Nancy Van Engen was next in age but played with us less often, mostly because we teased her, I think. Dick, the youngest Van Engen, was Katy's constant companion, just as Earl was mine, and spent many hours with us.

The Drexel cousins—Mary Edith, Ralph, and Dorothy—used the playhouse too, as did many of our friends in town.

It never seemed surprising to me that we had a playhouse, but it must have seemed extravagant to many of our neighbors. Most children had to make their own playhouses among the cedar trees or

The playhouse, our summer headquarters for make-believe, in 1933.

under drooping willows, building "pretend" walls of sticks and stones. We did that too, of course, just as we played cowboys-and-indians, rolled old tires, and learned to throw string-wound tops. We made hollyhock dolls, played hopscotch and run-sheep-run. It was all unsupervised and self-organized. We had never heard of "Little League" anything.

Shortly after the playhouse was built, Grandma and Grandpa Drexel moved into town from their crowded temporary dwelling on the ranch. And, best of all, they bought a house right across the street from us.

The last piece of furniture was hardly indoors on moving day when all three of us—Katy, Rie, and I—invaded their new home.

"May I help put the books away?"

"Does the organ still play?"

"May I have a peanut butter and honey sandwich, please, Grandma?"

"Grandpa, do the 'Plumpa' song for Katy—ple-e-ese?"

Grandpa probably was ready to sit down and rest a little without any invitation from us; at any rate, he didn't seem to mind the interruption and sat down on the nearest chair. Katy scrambled up on his lap and he began to sing in his thin, quavery voice this little song:

Hoppla, hoppla, Reiter!
Wenn er fallt, dann schreit er.
Fallt er in den Graben,
Fressen ihn die Raben;
Fallt er in den Sumpf,
Macht der Reiter . . . . plumps!

On the last word, "plumps," he spread his knees and Katy went plop on the floor. We all knew this would happen but it never seemed to get old.

"Again, Grandpa!" And again, and again, until Grandpa wore out and told us to go help Grandma a little bit.

The house seemed very grand indeed: It had two fireplaces, each with a dark brown marble hearth, large bay windows in the dining room and the front bedroom, dormers in each upstairs bedroom with windows that pushed out on hinges, and an attic with a floor in it. There was a cellar under the house and, out in the backyard, another root cellar dug into the hillside. It even had a beautiful indoor bathroom! And finally, it had a wide front porch that became a natural place to sit in the cool evenings; a place where grandchildren played all day; a place to rock in the cane-and-wicker chairs and dream or to listen to the birds conversing endlessly in the box elder trees; a place to watch the changing colors on the mountainsides and wonder about the world beyond. Now, instead of one house and yard to call home, we seemed to have two, and my memory always includes both places.

Grandma and Grandpa soon set to work to make their new grounds bloom with flowers, trees, and grass. They hauled rich black loam from Black Mesa in the honey truck and used it to build new flower beds. Blue spruce trees were planted along the back fence. Walls and terraces were built with large rocks gathered from the hillside behind the house. Grandpa laid pipe to several distant spots in the yard and installed a sprinkler system of his own design in the front lawn, all for ease in watering. By the second summer the yard began to bloom as never before.

But soon Grandpa had a real worry: He had discovered wild morning glory in the backyard in several spots. This is a weed that has been known to take over entire fields. It is tenacious, tough,

Grandma and Grandpa Drexel's home in Crawford, just across the street from our house, in the late 1930s.

resistant to poisons, and able to survive as long as a few roots remain undisturbed. Grandpa made up his mind to do battle.

First he fashioned a frame about a yard square and covered it with fine, strong wire mesh. Then he enlisted his sons to help him dig. They divided the backyard into small sections and took one section at a time. One dug the soil as deep as the morning glory roots were (and sometimes they went down nearly a foot). The other man pushed the soil through the screen and picked out all the roots, and the third worker removed the clean soil to a pile in another corner. After one section was cleared, the clean soil was returned to its home to start life over again.

It was painstaking, backbreaking labor and had to be done after the regular daily work and chores. It was an affirmation of the credo that if something is worth doing, it is worth doing well. Now, whenever I face a task that seems overwhelming, I say to myself "morning glories." The very thought of that project makes any job at hand seem easier.

Now that the grandparents lived in a real house again, they wanted to have the Victrola back. I knew we would miss it, but then, so had they during the last year! After the Victrola was gone

I began to practice the piano more and more. I had pushed ahead pretty much on my own and was beginning to read every piece of music I could find. On Sunday afternoons I tried playing all the hymns we had sung at Sunday school and church during the morning. It wasn't long before I could play most of them without a mistake, and I even began experimenting with some added notes, arranging it all to sound fuller and better. When I got one just right I would ask Grandpa to come over and listen.

No teacher ever listened with greater interest or intensity to my efforts. He didn't mind criticizing, but this always came in the form of questions, by asking me to justify my way of doing things. "Are you sure that chord fits the style of a hymn?" or "Can a congregation really sing that fast?" I knew that when I got a song to please him it was really right.

A few months after the new house in town had become home and their belongings had been settled in permanent places, Grandma and Grandpa received a very mysterious box. It came up on the stage from Hotchkiss and was so big the driver brought it right to the house and asked Daddy to help unload it.

"What's in it Grandma? Did you order it from the catalogue? Can we see it?" We were full of questions.

Grandma just smiled and said, "Come over after supper and we'll have it unpacked so you can see for yourself. It came from your great-aunts in Baltimore and is something very special."

It was a policy at our house that a meal wasn't finished until all the dishes were washed, dried, and put away, and you can bet this chore got done in record time that evening. Then we all raced across the road to see the contents of the big box.

What we found was Grandma and Grandpa carefully unpacking dishes! I was disappointed and started to pick one up to see what was so special about it.

"Just a minute, young lady," said Grandpa with a warning frown. "You'd better let me tell you about these so you'll know to treat them with respect. This is a set of china my father gave my mother when they were married in 1868. It was made and hand-painted in France and is very old. See the dainty little lavender flowers and the fine gold edging? And every piece has 'Theodore Haviland,

Limoges, France' printed on it." Then he handed me a small pitcher to hold and look at.

As I touched it and felt the smoothness of the fragile china I could really understand what the word "quality" means. This was the finest piece of real china I had ever seen. I set it down very carefully and just stared as piece after piece emerged from the box until a complete service for twelve had been unpacked and set out on the large dining room table.

"But why did Aunt Helene send it here?" asked Rie.

"Well," said Grandpa, "Aunt Helene and Aunt Katie are not so young anymore and they are going to move from the old house in Baltimore into a small apartment. There won't be any room there for these. Also, they want these heirloom dishes to be passed down in the Drexel family and we must have them here to do that."

So the Drexel family had an heirloom! I felt we must be very rich indeed. The Haviland china took its place in the cupboard with the glass doors and was used for special occasions like Christmas dinner or Ladies Aid meetings.

5. Depression Days

THE GREAT Depression of the 1930s is a part of world history. It is a part of Crawford's history too, and changed habits in every household. As a child I didn't know about a Depression. What I knew was that there seemed to be worried looks on the grown-ups' faces and serious chats in Grandpa's front bedroom office across the street.

Momma started going to the beauty parlor for her marcel once every two weeks instead of every week. I liked going with her because I could watch Mrs. Simmons put the finger waves in row on row, or stare at the new permanent-wave machine with its dozens of tentacles hanging down from a metal hood, like a Buck Rogers space contraption. When I tired of all that, I could peak into a large back room where Mr. Simmons operated the creamery—a sparkling clean place where ranchers brought milk, cream, and butterfat to be sold to a dairy farther down the valley. I liked the neat rows of cans and bottles and the odor of fresh milk and rich yellow cream.

As money became scarce, everyone tightened the proverbial belt. The creamery closed down. The feed and flour mill, down near Aunt Grace's house, cut back to half-production. Some farmers and ranchers let their fields go fallow and went to work in the coal mines beyond Paonia, thirty miles away.

Then came the morning when Daddy himself left home for a fruit-picking job in the orchards near Grand Junction. What a bad morning that was! Momma was cross—to hide her sadness and worry. The French toast got burned. Rie cried because Momma wouldn't smile.

"Why do you have to go, Daddy?" little Katy asked, with tears in her eyes.

"Well, Sweety, no one buys honey when times are hard, so we never did sell last summer's crop. I'll have to go earn some money so you can have pretty new shoes and things like that." I tried not to cry when we said good-bye.

Having Daddy gone was like living in a house with all the shades pulled down. Days dragged like sick snails. Happiness had fled beyond the horizon somewhere, and even Grandpa's brave whistle in the garden across the street couldn't lighten our mood.

Three weeks passed like this, and then Daddy came home. He detested being away. And, he said, he'd had an idea: He would learn to be an electrician. By now the new Rural Electrification Administration program had brought the power line to Crawford and everyone wanted to hook up. If he could learn how to do the wiring and become licensed, there would be plenty of work.

When school began, Momma boarded three of the teachers at our house and Grandma rented rooms to two of them in her upstairs bedrooms. And every evening Daddy studied the electric wiring manual. There wasn't much time for games or singing or reading a bedtime story, but at least we were all together, and we didn't complain.

Actually, the Crawford folks fared a good deal better than did thousands of people in the big cities. At least no one starved in Crawford. Nearly every family, even in town, had a large garden or fruit trees, a cow or pig or chickens. Folks shared and helped one another. Mr. Savage at the bank put off collecting on loans as long as possible. Mr. Wilson and Mr. Zeldenhuis, the grocers, and Mr. Welborn, the druggist, were very patient about the monthly bills and carried some people on their books for a year or more without complaining. Many people traded chicken feed for milk, eggs for potatoes, a few hours' work for some green vegetables, and so on.

I guess I knew we were poor, but then, almost everyone was poor. We had plenty to eat and never suffered in a physical way. The one bad memory I carried away from those years concerned the boxes from Baltimore that arrived each summer. They were filled with clothing the great-aunts thought Momma, Aunt Grace, and Grandma could remake for us. I knew that the wool things, the silks, and the knit goods were really very nice, even beautiful sometimes. But the idea of having to wear made-over things and hand-me-downs hurt my pride so much I felt like crying. If I complained, Momma just said, "Pride goeth before a fall, young lady." So I kept my bad feelings to myself and spent hours looking at the Montgomery Ward catalogue, wishing I could have some of those pretty things.

In 1933, during the worst of the Depression, Daddy faced a new dilemma: There wasn't any spare money and yet he had to find a way to build another bedroom for his family. Katy was three and had to move out of the crib. In the end he did what he found himself doing many times through the years—he went to the bank and took out a loan. And then some wonderful changes took place at our house. The roof was raised to accommodate an upstairs bedroom and a floored space for a Ping-Pong table. An indoor bathroom with a real tub and shower was built into a corner of the back porch next to the kitchen, and the house was wired for electricity. So now, instead of an outdoor privy and a tin tub beside the coal range and gas lamps with their white-hot wicks, we had a really modern house with all the nice things, just like people in magazine stories.

For me the whole thing was doubly exciting because the new bedroom was mine. Rie and Katy would have to share the double bed downstairs.

True, my new room had walls made of gunnysacks tacked to the studs, no ceiling between me and the rafters, a curtain for a door, and rough boards on the floor, but it was all mine. Now I could fix up this little room any way I wanted, lie on my bed and daydream without being spied on, write secrets in my diary in privacy. And it all came just in time, because I had fallen in love.

The object of my affection was a new boy, Chad Bushnel, whose family had just moved to Fruitland Mesa from Colorado Springs. Every girl in the third and fourth grade room fell for him from the first day of school. He dressed so elegantly! Instead of overalls he had on brown tweed knickers. His shoes were new and not at all dirty. And he was cute, with big brown eyes and carefully combed

Our house after the roof was raised. The Jitney is at the far left, the playhouse is in the gully at the right, and the icehouse and barn are in back.

hair, and had very nice manners. And his name! Chad—that was so romantic! Most of the girls spent every recess giggling and making eyes at this new charmer. But I thought I knew a better way to get his attention: I would make Willie trade seats with me so I could sit right across the aisle from Chad. Willie was a bit slow-witted and couldn't always keep up, but he stayed in school anyway. He never caused any trouble and he usually passed because the teachers didn't know how else to help him. During recess one day I cornered Willie and asked him about trading seats.

"Uh, uh—sure—I guess so." Willie blushed from the top button of his denim shirt to the tips of his big ears and fled.

Then I went to see Miss Robinson. "Please, Miss Robinson, may I change seats with Willie? I can't see the front blackboard very well because the light shines wrong where I am. Willie says it's okay."

Miss Robinson looked at me with a very funny expression, considered the proposal for a minute, and said, "I'll arrange it after lunch today." All the girls looked green with envy, but since none of them had thought of the seat-trading idea they couldn't very well say anything.

About a week later Chad passed a note to me. Inside the folded note was a gold-colored ring. It was too big to wear anywhere except on my thumb, but every recess I put it on and made sure Chad saw it. School took on the aura of heaven on earth.

Third grade was fun in some other ways, too. There were the colored-chalk decorations. Miss Robinson had paper patterns something like player-piano rolls with designs punched into them of lines of tiny dots. We held the paper against the blackboard and patted or rubbed different colors of chalk dust into the holes. Then, when we took the paper away, there would be a bird, or green leaves, or white berries on a vine, or whatever. Sometimes when we got to school in the morning there would be a whole new picture on the board as if it had just put itself there by magic in the night. Sometimes Miss Robinson worked on new designs during recess and would let us watch or help her hold the paper or make chalk dust.

One recess, while Jean Kraai and I were busily making dust by scribbling yellow chalk onto the blackboard and then rubbing it off into erasers, we heard Jimmy Ward and Dale Drake talking out in the hall.

"Let's do it tomorrow." Short silence, then "Can you git Oscar to bring some peanuts too? That ought to be enough." Then, "Maybe we oughta tell Betty so she can git the girls to bring some too."

Jean and I looked at each other and giggled. Peanut shower! Had Miss Robinson heard? She was way over at the other end of the room making pumpkin designs. She couldn't have heard that far.

The next day, bags of unshelled peanuts were shoved into desks along with tablets and books and pencils. "We'll start throwing at the beginning of spelling" was the message that made the rounds. Chad had no idea what we were talking about, so it was with absolute astonishment that he saw all of us start throwing peanuts at Miss Robinson just as she turned her back to write the new spelling words on the blackboard. Peanut showers were not new to Miss Robinson, however. She knew just what to do. First she pretended to be terribly surprised, then she laughed and told us to put our books away. We picked up all the nuts, shelled them, ate them, sang a few songs, and made a real party of it. Chad gave me half of his peanuts and winked at me as we sang "School Days."

I can't imagine that teachers liked peanut showers, but they all tolerated one a year. Woe to any students who tried to sneak in a second one, though. That would rate a trip to the principal's office, where, it was rumored, a special paddle was kept for such offenders.

Thanksgiving was almost upon us when it finally became apparent to the school fathers that money was going out fast but not coming in. There just wasn't any money left, to be quite honest, and no place to find any. The school board reluctantly decided to stop the school year short at the end of January and to plan another five-month term for the following year, hoping that by 1935 they could afford a full nine months again. So it was that it took us all two years to complete our grades.

I wouldn't have minded if something even worse hadn't happened. Chad's parents decided to go back to Colorado Springs! Here I had been expecting life to stretch ahead in eternal bliss, and suddenly, just like that, it seemed all over. I was devastated. It's all very well for grown-ups to dismiss such special friendships as "mere puppy love," but I know better. There's nothing mere about it. It hurts, like a lump in the stomach or the aching of flu. The new upstairs bedroom became a haven for my broken heart.

6. Summertime

IF WINTER comes can spring be far behind? So goes the familiar saying. But it seldom applies in Colorado's mountains. When winter comes there, spring follows *far* behind.

Mostly there's mud. All through March and April, in fact. Snow turns to slush and disappears. Icicles, which once seemed to be permanent glass decorations, drip themselves away to nothing. The adobe soil becomes a sticky gray goo and a challenge to every driver. The unpaved country roads are either slick or gummy. In those early days, before gravel or paving, special "mud days" were reserved on the school calendar for closings because of impassable roads.

Spring usually shows itself by May, finally, and as children, we celebrated by making May baskets. These were as varied as our imaginations and made of construction paper decorated with bits of lace, ribbon, cut-out designs, or crayon drawings. We filled them with whatever wildflowers we could find around town. Then, just before dark on May Day, we carried them to certain ladies' front doors, knocked, and hid close-by to watch. The idea was to choose someone who would not only appreciate the pretty little basket but might also reward us with a piece of candy. A German lady by the name of Miss Peitch made hand-dipped chocolate candies for May Day, and every child in town visited her.

The spring of 1934 must have been hard for the Drexel grown-ups quite apart from mud and slush. Last year's honey was still unsold. There weren't any odd jobs to be had, either. Grandpa remained optimistic, however. He was a Democrat and Roosevelt was now president. Already, new and creative programs had begun to relieve the worst conditions in the cities. "Things will get better now," he said.

Daddy seldom argued with his father, but they disagreed thoroughly on the subject of politics.

"How can you like Roosevelt when he supports the liquor crowd?" In Daddy's book, "liquor crowd" meant the devil with horns plus national disaster.

Grandpa would frown and reply curtly, "Remember, you have Roosevelt to thank for the Rural Electrification Act. You wouldn't have any wiring jobs at all if it weren't for that."

"Electrification would have come regardless of who won the election," argued Daddy. "And another thing, all these welfare programs seem socialistic to me, just not compatible with the free enterprise system."

"Clarence, you wouldn't feel that way if you lived in a city and had to depend on the whim of an employer for your living. You just don't know what it's like to be a common laborer."

But Grandpa, Daddy, and Uncle Frank were soon too busy to sit around arguing. The dandelions bloomed, lilacs spread their nostalgic fragrance, seed puffs from the cottonwood trees floated everywhere, and May melted away to summer. With the warm sun and summer flowers came the active season for bees and their keepers.

The techniques and tools of the profession of beekeeping change through the years, but the basics are the same. The first job is to remove the boxes of straw that have covered and protected the hives during the long, cold winter. This can take several days for a large operation such as the Drexel enterprise. As the bees become active, they clean their hives by pushing dead bees and broken beeswax cells out. The good beekeeper helps the tiny workers in this job and puts new honeycomb foundations in the hive. Then the busy worker bees go about the business of making honeycomb cells and filling them full of flower nectar.

In the meantime, a very special bee, called the queen, is busy filling a section of comb with tiny eggs. One of these eggs, when it becomes a larva, is selected as a princess bee and fed something

Caleb Maher, his daughter Ella, and a friend transporting honey to the railroad in 1910.

called "royal jelly." When the princess bee grows into a new young queen bee, an exciting thing happens. The old queen gathers her faithful workers and leaves the hive to find a new home. The princess is still in her waxen cell when this happens. But she will, in a matter of a few days, come out and take possession of her hive. All around her cell are other cells with larvae that will emerge when she does and become her workers. *Voilà!* A new colony of bees is born.

A swarm of bees can be frightening to a bystander. Bees fly in a mass, or cloud, that makes a threatening hum as it moves above the ground. They follow their queen as she hunts for a spot to land, usually on a branch of a tree. The workers form a bushel-sized cluster, like a huge bunch of grapes, around the queen and become very quiet. They wait, unmoving, until the scout bees have found a suitable hole for a new home. Swarms sometimes rest in a ball for several hours, seeming to enjoy the peace and sunshine after the frenzy of the flight.

It is during this short, quiet resting phase that the beekeeper has a chance to retrieve his bees. Sometimes an observant passerby will see the swarm and call the beekeeper. Sometimes the apiarist will find the near-empty hive himself. He must then stop whatever he's doing and go immediately to hunt for the missing bees.

A typical bee swarm.

How does a beekeeper get this swarm back? Well, he takes a large basket or box to put the bees in and carries a ladder for climbing the tree. He may not even need a veil because the bees are quite docile during the waiting period. All he has to do is give the tree branch a quick shake and the great cluster of bees will fall passively into the container. A few bees might fly around curiously, but they won't trouble anyone. The whole swarm can now be carried back to the apiary and introduced to an empty hive. They won't know the difference.

If a swarm manages to escape, or if a new young queen doesn't live to form her own colony, then the beekeeper will order a new queen from a supply house. How I used to hate to be the one who picked up the mail on a day when I found, in our box at the post office, a small wire cage with a live and angry queen bee in it. I knew the queen had no stinger, but it still was disconcerting to carry that buzzing, fuming little lady home in my hands.

It would take another book to describe the work of a beekeeper during the rest of the honey-making season. Suffice it to say that from May to October the apiarist is busy all day, nearly every day. He adds upper stories, called supers, to the hives; he removes full combs of honey and replaces them with ready-made foundations for new combs; he extracts and stores the honey; he inspects the hives for diseased bees, and when he finds them destroys the whole colony with cyanide and burns the hive. The work is physically tiring, but to most apiarists it is so rewarding that no other job in the world could match it. Bees are fascinating creatures—a mixture of amazing intelligence and instinct. Working with them can be an adventurous pilgrimage.

While June meant hard-work time for our father, it meant vacation time for us youngsters. It was also a signal for going barefoot. It was a ritual: June first, no shoes. I didn't like going barefoot, but for two or three days I pretended I did. After that I reverted to acting like a girl and put my shoes back on. Boys went ahead and toughened their feet or else had to endure the taunts of "Yah, yah, he's a sissy!"

Summer was lovely—birds chattering all around, silvery leaves on poplar trees glittering and shivering in the breeze, the heady perfume of the Russian olive trees turning the air thick with sweetness.

One could lie on the cool green lawn and listen to the noisy creek below while looking for pictures in the clouds. Or go hunting for arrowheads up on the hillside, then cool off by wading in the ditch near the house.

Most mornings I would wake to the sound of sprinklers swishing away busily either in our yard or across the street. In that land of scarce and precious water, each household was allowed just so many watering hours every other day, so most people watered their yards and gardens in the early part of the day before the hot sun could evaporate much of it.

I woke at dawn one June day feeling an uncommon sense of excitement. But why? The usual fresh-smelling water sprayed the front lawn. Birds twittered as always in the poplar tree. Then I remembered: Today I was going to climb Young's Peak! I had never done it, but all the older kids had, and I had waited impatiently to be old enough to go to the top of the big hill that rises directly behind Crawford. Actually, the town sits on the side of Young's Peak and is nestled on a narrow flattened spot where several roads converge. When I was smaller I had heard people talk about going up to the "sea" on the peak. I wondered and wondered how an ocean, or even a tiny lake, could be up there on the ridge of that dry brown hill. By the time I was a fourth-grader I knew better—the "C" was a large letter formed with whitewashed rocks. Every small town near us had such a letter on a nearby hill, but we thought Crawford's was the best because our hill was the highest. Now I would see the C up close!

Peggy Hillman and her big brother, Kenneth, led the expedition. Peggy was four years older than I, but she played with all of us most every day. Momma packed a lunch in a paper sack and Kenneth had a canvas water bag slung on his back, so we were well provisioned. And off we went!

At first the climbing was easy. All we had to do was watch out for cactus or slippery rocks. After a bit, though, the hill began to get steep. In fact, it seemed to be almost straight up. And *all* the rocks seemed slippery—three steps up and two slips down, over and over, until I wondered if it were really possible to reach the top. I later learned that Young's Peak is an interesting place to geologists because of those slippery rocks, which are known as shale, some of it containing oil. And if you know what to look for you can find fossils of shells from an ancient ocean that *did* once cover this land. But to me, at that moment, the hill seemed to be an insurmountable peak of treacherous flat stones.

When at last we did reach the top I sat down and just stared. What a sight! We seemed to be on top of the world, gazing down on everything. My house looked like a toy, and the schoolhouse was not much bigger. I could see for miles in all directions: the high blue mountains to the east; the fertile valleys and ranches south beyond the town; the endless desert westward to the horizon; the bald, salt-encrusted badlands of clay soil, called the "dobies," north of us. This was worth the climb all right—every torturous minute of it. No matter that my legs ached and my head pounded. Let my feet hurt! Who cared that my socks were full of cactus!

We ate our lunch and drank the cool water from Kenneth's bag and I felt very grown-up. Going down looked easy enough—just walk down, or maybe slide a little. Because we had climbed up the east side, we decided to come down the south face so we could go right past the C, even though it did look fiercely steep. Five steps or so later I wished we'd made some other decision. I found myself on my back, sliding at a distressing rate and unable to stop—past a tree, barely missing a clump of cactus, bumpity-bump over slide-rock—and finally coming to rest against a friendly, solid piñon tree. My elbow was skinned, my pants were torn, and I had a sudden flash of insight: I knew now why the high school boys were never punished when they played hooky from school every spring to come up here and whitewash the C. Anyone who could carry buckets of paint up to this spot deserved a day off from school!

It was well along in June that same summer, after the roads finally dried out, that Grandma suggested a trip to Black Canyon. "Let's take the honey truck," she said, "so we can take all the kids." Even Grandpa decided to go along.

The honey truck was a Dodge that had been bought back in the twenties and had served the Drexel families for many years. Of course honey was transported in it, as well as all the other paraphernalia involved in beekeeping. Benches were built along each side of the truck bed so as many as ten people could ride in it, too. It had heavy wire mesh on the sides, a strong metal roof, and canvas

The Drexel families' Dodge honey truck.

curtains that could be rolled up in fair weather or put down to enclose the truck. It bounced over all the rutted, rocky roads with ease—a really sturdy vehicle.

Black Canyon would be one of the wonders of the world if it were well known. Wallace Henson, a geologist, studied the canyon for a number of years and said, "Some are longer, some are deeper, some are narrower, and a few have walls as steep. But no other canyon in North America combines the depth, narrowness, sheerness, and somber countenance of the Black Canyon of the Gunnison." Called "black" because the sun rarely reaches the bottom, it is a narrow chasm half a mile deep and only eleven hundred feet across from rim to rim. The Gunnison River roars through the bottom of the canyon, constantly digging it deeper and deeper. In many places the bottom is only forty feet across, and the water responds to this constriction by forming rapids and whirlpools. You can stand on the rim and look down—straight down—to the depths below, so deep they lie in constant shadow while the thunder of the river reverberates and echoes back and forth across those vertical walls. You can feel, in the midst of this constant roar, a strange sense of overwhelming peace and realize that this scene has been here, just like this, for thousands of years and will remain this way for thousands more.

As a child I was terrified of Black Canyon. Now, as an adult, I see its beauty. I stand in awe and feel drawn to it like a needle to a magnet.

From an airplane the canyon looks like a jagged cut in the earth's crust, as though an ancient earthquake had split the ground open. Or perhaps Nature, in a moment of caprice, decided to open the planet's innards just enough to tantalize us. Geologists use terms like "schist" and "gneiss" to describe the walls. Ordinary folks are more apt to say "dark" or "granite" walls. The poets say it best when they use words such as "somber" and "forbidding."

Nowadays a fairly good road, paved most of the way, takes sightseers in a leisurely twenty minutes from Crawford to the entrance of the Black Canyon National Monument and the scenic Rim Road. Back in the thirties the road was a bumpy single-lane trail that seemed to follow the latest sheep run. It led from the settled portions of Fruitland Mesa to the remote, higher mesa land filled with sage, piñon, cedar, and grass. Jackrabbits, coyotes, and deer roamed the countryside, sometimes having to share their home with herds of grazing sheep. If it was dry enough to take a vehicle through, it was invariably dusty. In fact, the odor of sage and dust are inseparable in my memory of that place.

When the truck finally pulled up at the gate where the road ended, Momma and Aunt Grace organized the kids in twos, and each pair walked with an adult so we wouldn't get lost on the trail out to the edge. It seemed to take a long time to walk that trail, but I was so afraid of what I was going to see when we got there that I never felt any urge to hurry.

At last we could hear the muffled roar of the water, and then the trail ended abruptly at the edge of the canyon. I wanted to see over the edge, yet I was afraid to just walk out to it and look over. So I got down on my hands and knees and crawled; then, with Daddy holding my feet, I lay flat on my stomach and peered over the edge. There was the river, a tiny ribbon half a mile below— straight down. Boulders the size of houses looked like pebbles. Canyon swallows wheeled and soared through the shadowy depths. The noise of the river roared up from the bottom. Rie was just as frightened as I was and held tightly to Momma's hand the whole time. Mary Edith and Ralph pretended they weren't afraid at all and

An aerial view of the Black Canyon, taken sometime in the 1930s. Photograph by Davis Studio, Hotchkiss, Colorado.

got almost to the rim standing up. Little Katy and Dorothy were just toddlers, so Momma tied them with a piece of rope to a nearby tree so they couldn't wander off.

It was Grandma who worried everyone most, though. She was fearless. And there was so much to see—a glistening piece of mica here, a beautiful rock filled with quartz chips there, a serviceberry bush full of tiny white blossoms, a gaudy Indian paintbrush over yonder. It didn't seem to matter to her that a particular plant she was interested in was perilously close to a crumbling piece of rock right on the edge of the canyon.

"You'd better come on back from there, Old Girl," Grandpa said with a worried frown.

"Oh, really! I'm not in any danger. I just want a sprig of this wild daisy." And Grandma blithely pursued the elusive little branch.

"Ella! You get back here right now." When Grandpa spoke in that tone everyone obeyed, even Grandma. And she reluctantly left the pretty posies where they were.

That night I dreamed I was trying to reach a beautiful bush full of silver and gold leaves and I fell off the edge of the canyon. I woke up on the floor and then was afraid to go back to sleep.

A few years later Daddy came home for supper one clear summer evening grinning from ear to ear.

"Bet you can't guess what I did this afternoon," he teased.

"Did you get stung by a bumblebee?"

"I'll bet you wrecked the truck." Katy tended to favor really gruesome ideas.

"Nope," said Daddy, "I flew over Black Canyon in an airplane!"

"Clarence!" Momma's face had suddenly gone all white and she sat down weakly in the rocking chair.

"Yep," continued Daddy. "A fella from Grand Junction called and asked if I'd like to go with him while he took some aerial photos of Gould Reservoir for the *Grand Junction Sentinel.* When we got up there the air was so quiet he said this would be a good time to fly over the canyon, too. Boy, that was quite a ride! Especially when we swooped down *into* the Canyon a little way. Felt just like a bird, diving and floating around out there."

"Oh, Clarence," Momma said again, even weaker this time. "Please don't ever do that again."

"Why not? That was the most fun I've ever had!" And Daddy smiled again with a dreamy look in his eye.

Strangely enough, this mild-mannered man, who could hardly be described as daring, did enjoy the thrill of flying, and he continued to love it all his life. He never understood how anyone could possibly be afraid of such pleasure.

Momma, on the other hand, *was* afraid of flying—and of bees, of going fast in cars, of Katy's constant tree-climbing. You could make a long list of things Momma felt fearful about. She could be counted on to dwell on the worst parts of any situation. Sometimes she would be cross or would burst out crying for no reason whatsoever.

Describing my mother isn't that simple, however. She was also quick-witted, clever, and had a marvelous sense of humor. When something funny happened, Momma's laugh rang out like bells and her face became really pretty. A picture I've seen of her as a coed during her one year of college shows her to have been a real beauty with thick brown hair and lustrous brown eyes. She always was

My parents, Clarence and Esther Drexel, about 1941.

proud of her trim, well-shaped figure and lovely legs and ankles. I've been told by those who remember her as a girl that she was vivacious, full of fun, and very ambitious.

It wasn't until many years later that anyone in the family really understood what altered her personality so drastically. The depression she had first suffered when Katy was a baby came back to haunt the rest of her days. She lived through succeeding episodes of that nameless panic and dread, dullness of feeling, and inability to think and plan. Even when the depression wasn't present, for her there was always the fear that it would strike again. As I look back and realize how much she accomplished as a wife and mother, I wonder what kind of dynamo she might have been if she hadn't been forced to spend so much energy battling that baffling illness.

7. Autumn

"WHEN THE moon comes over the mountain . . ." Kate Smith's voice flowed from the radio on the shelf, its mellow sound adding warmth to the circle of light where the family gathered round the dining room table one September evening. Momma sat with Katy in her lap while she read a story to Rie about Winnie the Pooh and Piglet. A cricket, hidden under one of the table legs, went *chir-up, chir-up, chir-up* every few seconds. I tried not to listen to all the interesting distractions as I turned the pages of *Time* magazine looking for a punchy item to take to current events at school. Maybe the feature story about Hitler, the little German with the square mustache, would be good. Or how about the Dionne quintuplets? Imagine raising five babies at once! Diapers, lines and lines full every day, bottles lined up in the kitchen like a factory, commotion—what if they all cried at once? Would you just walk down the row of baskets, jiggle each baby for a minute, and sing a lullaby real loud? Even twins were a lot of trouble—at least that's what Aunt Jennie Te Grotenhuis said about her twins, Madeline and Evelyn.

Daddy sat at the desk in the living room on the other side of the shelf that held the radio. He seemed to be adding long lists of numbers and coming out with unsatisfactory answers. Every now and then he would crumple up a sheet of paper, look disturbed, and start a fresh list. He wasn't often visibly unhappy—his naturally

ready grin and contented disposition usually hid whatever dissatis-
faction he felt. Although not as handsome as his brother Frank,
he was a good-looking man with brown eyes and dark hair. Not
tall, but not short either, he had a presence of quiet authority that
made it easy to look up to him. Because he neither hunted nor fished
and wasn't a sporting man, he was regarded as a rather odd duck
by some of the men in the community, but he was well respected
by most.

Now it was easy to see that he was troubled. I had caught a
bit of conversation between him and Grandpa that afternoon.

"—we'll probably lose money this first year if we do it," warned
Grandpa.

"We've had only this one bid for the honey crop so far and it's
too low to give us a profit. The beeswax will make a little all right,
but I doubt if we can hope for any better offers on the honey,"
Daddy said in a worried way.

"Frank says 'absolutely no deal.' He wants no part of it. So, if
we join the Sioux Bee Coop he'll probably drop out of the company."

"Well, he hasn't been very happy being in it. Maybe this is the
best for him and for us."

"He told me he'd had an offer from Independent Lumber in
Hotchkiss—bookkeeper, I think."

"Sounds good! I'll think it over a bit more. You say we must
decide by Thursday at the latest?"

Daddy's figures must have convinced him that the company
couldn't survive alone. Grandpa Drexel sold the honey to, and
joined, the Sioux Bee Honey Company in Iowa, one of the many
cooperatives that sprang up during the Depression. The Frank H.
Drexel and Sons Company ceased to exist. From then on the honey
would automatically be sold to Sioux Bee regardless of the price,
but it would always be sold—no more waiting for the highest bidder
or taking the chance of losing out completely.

No one talked about it much. In true Drexel fashion, the men
just went on with the job at hand and mourned silently, if at all.
There probably wasn't time enough to dwell on regrets anyhow,
because two men were now doing the work of three. Also, Daddy
was picking up many more wiring contracts, now that folks knew
he could do a good job and was trustworthy.

October and fall arrived together that year—as always, a beautiful time in Colorado. The sky was a seamless blue dome, the trees shades of gold bedizened with gaudy splashes of red and orange. Dark green pine and spruce scattered among the flame-colored hardwoods served to add even more intensity to the panorama, and the white bark of the quaking aspen trees made everything shimmer as if lined with silver. On the mesas there was an overall aroma of dry sage and dust, and higher up in the hills the spruce trees and fallen leaves mingled in a lovely woodsy smell. The air was quiet, a soft haze lay over the land, streams merely murmured now and then—everything seemed at peace.

Then, as now, fall was a busy time for ranchers. The sheepherders brought their flocks down to lower and warmer feeding grounds, so the roads were often filled with masses of bleating woolly creatures. A car was quite useless in such a situation, and one could only stop and wait for the tide of sheep to pass. Cowboys packed their saddlebags and headed for the roundup in the high country where the cattle had been feeding all summer. This is probably the cowboy's favorite time. It's so beautiful up in the hills. And being on horseback is the finest of all possible ways to travel there. Farmers hurried to finish the last cutting of alfalfa and fill the barns with hay. Women finished the last of the canning and helped the men gather carrots and potatoes to be stored in big boxes of dirt waiting in their cellars.

For Grandpa Drexel and Daddy, this was bee-packing time. Each hive in every yard had to be covered with a large box and the space between hive and box had to be packed with straw. Then, each colony of bees was given a supply of honey to last through the inactive cold months. Not every beekeeper in western Colorado did this. Those whose first priority was to make money simply moved their bees to a warmer location in states south of Colorado, taking their families with them or, in some cases, going alone.

Some said that Clarence Drexel wasn't ambitious; but if Daddy had wanted to be wealthy he wouldn't have become a beekeeper in the first place. When he graduated from the Agricultural College at Fort Collins with a degree in forestry, he found that the only jobs available were as clerks or assistants of some sort in various offices. Being cooped up indoors was not for him. He had simply decided he'd rather join his father's business where he could be a free man. He must have had moments of regret when the needs and desires of his family exceeded his ability to provide for them, but I doubt if he could have lived so contentedly in any other setting.

October meant not only harvest but also piles of leaves to play in, fresh cider, roller-skating on the short stretch of cement sidewalk in front of the church, the World Series, herds of cattle being driven through town, tired and dirty cowboys lounging in front of the pool hall or the drugstore, and, finally, Halloween.

In those days Halloween was truly the trickster's holiday. The fun-loving boys in town spent considerable time planning some kind of devilry. One year they stole the school bell and deposited it at the bottom of a cliff in Smith Fork Canyon. Another year a much-hated schoolteacher came back from a weekend away to find the chimney of her house plugged up and black soot over everything inside. Quite obviously, the town fathers were a bit tense as each October 31 approached.

The day before one Halloween, Daddy had seen Jimmy Ward and two other mischievous boys in a huddle behind the bank. He knew something was afoot but had no notion what. He mentioned it at the post office, where all the gossip and news collected, and next day when he got home he put the truck in the garage behind the house, padlocked the coal house, icehouse, and cellar doors, and generally secured everything he could. All was quiet at bedtime, though, so he relaxed a little and decided he had wronged those boys with bad thoughts. Nevertheless, he left his shoes and pants beside the bed, just in case.

As he told it later, he was awakened about midnight when he heard somebody swearing out by the driveway. Then there was a creaking noise—something to do with the gate—and the sound of scuffling feet. Daddy jumped out of bed in a flash, pulled his pants on right over his nightshirt, hastily tied his shoes, and ran for the front door. He got there just in time to see Jimmy Ward and two other boys lift the gate from its hinges and start to drag it down the street, and he gave chase. The boys dropped the gate and took off through the neighbor's yard toward the church with Daddy close behind. In spite of their head start, he actually gained on them until they got to the cemetery fence. Over they went with

Daddy on their tail, when his nightshirt, which had been flopping along behind him, got caught in the barbed wire and stopped him cold. The boys never even glanced back; they just ran as if the devil himself were after them.

Next day, when Daddy went downtown for the mail, Uncle Bill grinned and said, "I hear some fellow was running around town last night in nothing but a nightshirt." And Ray Zeldenhuis in the grocery store teased him a bit about trying to recapture his youth. He just grinned back and said he figured a few boys probably were as tired as he was this morning. They certainly hadn't stopped with gate-stealing; every store window in town had been well soaped, and an old junk car was parked in the middle of the street in front of the bank.

A few days later Daddy came to dinner with the news: "The gypsies are back! They sure are late this year; they ought to be getting to a warmer climate by now. I'll bet those tents are a bit chilly at night." Considering that we had already had one light frost, I agreed wholeheartedly and wondered what it must be like to live the way those strange people did.

That very afternoon there was a knock at the front door. "Could you folks spare a quart of milk for our baby? And if you have any extra eggs, we'd really appreciate just a couple or so." The two women standing there were black-haired and dark-eyed and wore bright bandanas around their necks. Long, full, dirty skirts, scruffy shoes, and tattered shawls completed the look of weary travelers. They were so polite and so needy-looking that a person just couldn't turn them away. Momma fixed up a sack with a jar of milk, some eggs, and a loaf of bread fresh from the oven. With much polite bowing and murmuring the women withdrew and disappeared down the hill.

Daddy had said their camp was down beside the creek near the bridge. The creekbed widens there, and from the middle of the summer on, when the water is low, most of the area is a parklike spot with cottonwood trees, grass, and pebbly beaches all along the edge of the stream.

I felt happy about our good deed until suppertime, when Momma came raging up from the cellar.

"Just guess what those gypsies did! While those women were up here begging from us somebody else was down cellar robbing us.

One of the bee yards at The Ranch in winter.

They've taken canned tomatoes and peaches and jelly and pickles.
I'm *sure* some of the potatoes and carrots are gone, too. Honestly,
Clarence, it's a crime!"

"Now, Ma, you know they do this to somebody every year.
Guess it's our turn this year." And Daddy tried to make her laugh
with a funny face.

"But it's *wrong* to steal—you *know* it is. I'd have given them
more gladly, but it's not right to just take things; it's just not right."
Momma simply couldn't help feeling indignant about the injustice
of it, even though at the same time she felt sorry for those poor
homeless people.

The gypsy clan stayed for three or four days and then just disappeared. As always, no one knew exactly where they came from,
where they were going, or why they lived that way. The Crawford
folks just accepted them as they were and granted their right to
live any way they chose.

By the time the gypsies had come and gone, winter was knock-
ing at the door. Each morning we could see a dusting of snow on
the mountains gradually sneaking lower and lower down to the
foothills. The water in the birdbath at Grandpa's froze solid. The
men drained the watering hoses and stored them for the winter.
Now it was time for indoor pleasures and new dreams.

8. Holiday Time

EACH HOLIDAY had a special flavor in our family and a special setting
that hardly varied from year to year. Thanksgiving was always celebrated at the home of Gramma Den Beste's sister, Aunt Jennie
Te Grotenhuis. Aunt Jennie and Uncle Ed lived on a mesa west
of Hotchkiss and had a family every bit as large as the Den Bestes.
Thanksgiving was not a single-family gathering but a reunion of
aunts, uncles, cousins, and second cousins; it was a huge banquet
of turkey with the usual additions of casseroles, pies, and cakes—
the best cooking all those Dutch women could produce. It was a
grand and rousing songfest with music of all kinds, from hymns
to Stephen Foster favorites to a splendid rendition of "Kitten on
the Keys" at the piano. A special part of each of these family gatherings was the singing of the Doxology as a blessing before the meal.
I've never heard richer harmony than those people brought to this
simple hymn of thanks. It was, in short, an occasion to be savored
and remembered from year to year.

It didn't occur to me that Thanksgiving Day could be celebrated
any other way. In my innocence I supposed everyone had a Thanksgiving feast like ours. The truth is, of course, that there were many
lonesome souls in the Crawford country who had no family at all:
traveling cowboys who spent their free time at the pool hall drinking beer and swapping yarns, mountaineers who lived like hermits

and didn't mark the day at all, settlers who had come to Crawford alone to escape some tragedy and had never acquired a family.

By far the most important holiday of the year, however, was Christmas. The setting in this case was a kaleidoscope of places and events. There was the program at the school gym where each grade put on a skit or play or sang some traditional Christmas songs. There was a big star Mr. Savage had erected on the top of "Ski Hill." It could be seen all up and down the valley. Mr. Welborn decorated the drugstore windows with silver tinsel rope and fancy bottles of perfume and lilac water and hand-tooled leather belts and wallets. Mr. Zeldenhuis put cotton batting to simulate snow in the window of the grocery store and laid out Valencia oranges, pecans, and packages of dates on it. Mr. Savage put little shiny metal savings banks in the bank window and strung colored lights around the door. Everybody got busy making presents, ordering things from the "Monkey Ward" catalogue, baking goodies, and trimming their trees.

Daddy always brought two trees down from whatever place in the mountains he had spotted months before. Often, he pruned and trimmed these trees as they grew so they would be nearly perfect. One cedar tree would be placed in the corner of our living room, and the other, the bigger one, went into Grandpa's living room. On went the pretty baubles and the foil icicles saved from year to year, and finally the little candles were placed in tiny holders that clipped onto the branches. Then every evening for the two weeks the tree stayed up, we sat for a little while after supper and watched Momma and Daddy light the candles and oh-ed and ah-ed as we admired their handiwork. Such a glory! Such a miracle of beauty! When finally those little lights were extinguished we felt as though we had just made a trip to fairyland.

The climax of all the preparation was Christmas Eve, when the whole community gathered at the church for a program of Christmas stories, carols, and, most exciting of all, the appearance of Santa Claus. For weeks and weeks all the Sunday school classes had been frantically rehearsing parts for the manger-scene play, for special songs, poems, and readings. Mrs. Brownell, the preacher's wife, was in charge of all this, and she worked for absolute perfection of performance.

Came the big evening, and the church was filled to capacity; extra chairs were brought in and placed as close to the potbellied stove as could be tolerated. Folks from way up in Onion Valley, near Black Mesa, families from out on Missouri Flats at the base of Needle Rock, farmers from the lower country on Crawford Mesa —the whole countryside was there to celebrate Christmas and welcome Santa Claus.

One year, when I was about five, my class had a song prepared with an introductory reading. My classmate Earl had been chosen to recite the reading because he was so good at memorizing things. Mrs. Brownell had drawn lines on the floor in white chalk to let us know just where to stand, and there was a special line in front for Earl. We felt pretty confident as the musical introduction started and we marched up on the stage and took our places. When the music stopped, Earl was supposed to begin his poem. Well, the music stopped and we waited, but there was silence—Earl seemed to be studying his shoes. Uncertainly, the pianist played the introduction again. Nothing happened. Finally Earl looked up at Mrs. Brownell in complete puzzlement and said, "I can't find the chalk mark!" After a moment of hushed silence a sort of whisper seemed to sweep the audience, and then it exploded in laughter. Earl, happy that he had pleased the crowd so much, waved to his mother and father, and then the rest of us started to wave to our families, too. The audience reacted with new gales of laughter. Order was restored only when Mrs. Brownell marched up on the stage and led us off to our seats.

And now it was time for the big event. Santa Claus should arrive any minute now. Listen carefully! Yes, we could hear sleigh bells somewhere off near the annex room beyond those doors at the side of the sanctuary. Then there was a stamping of feet, someone shouted to Donner and Blitzen, and the door flew open. In came a big, fat-bellied man dressed all in red with a long white beard. There was snow on his boots and he had a huge gunnysack slung on his back.

In a loud voice that sounded just like Ol Lewis down at the butcher shop, Santa said, "Ho, ho, ho! Greetings from the North Pole!" Then he told stories about how many places he had been and how busy he was going to be all night until I could hardly stand it. Finally he set the sack down and began to extract the contents. Little packages for the preacher, the mayor, each schoolteacher— on and on—and at last there were little bundles of candy all tied up

in bright ribbons, enough so each child in the audience got one.
When the sack was quite empty, Santa threw a gay wave to the
crowd and stomped back out to his sleigh. Oh, it was there all right!
You could hear those sleigh bells getting dimmer and dimmer somewhere beyond the annex.

As we got older and Santa's performance lost its fascination,
we found that the caroling group that toured town after the program was just as thrilling as the earlier make-believe had been. We
wrapped up in heavy coats, mittens, caps, and overshoes and walked
all over Crawford singing our favorite carols. The cold snow crackled
under our boots. The streetlights made glowing spots in the dark.
Lighted trees glittered at windows, and sometimes people waved
from their doorways. The air was still and the sound of our voices
carried all up and down the street. What a perfect way to celebrate
Christ's birthday!

Next morning Momma and Daddy got up extra early so they
would have the fires lit, the house all cozy warm, and the outdoor
chores done in order to be ready for the fun when we woke up.
First came breakfast, featuring the Christmas cake called *stollen,*
which had been baked by Grandpa and Grandma Drexel. This is
a traditional German holiday bread filled with currants, raisins,
citron, and nuts and covered with a frosting of butter, cinnamon,
and sugar—absolutely delicious. Finally, after the dishes were done
and the fires had been replenished, we settled down to the long-
awaited presents. Most of them had already been shaken and felt
until the wrappings looked weary and worn, but one little group
always appeared mysteriously sometime during the Christmas Eve
program. These always had Grandma's and Grandpa's names on
them, I noticed, but because the whole family went to the program
I never quite figured out how they got those presents delivered.

Then came the big holiday dinner across the road at Grandpa's
house. It was a festive time and a festive place. Both fireplaces were
burning merrily, making the rooms warm and pleasant. The big
tree held center stage at the window. It was decorated with the special
ornaments from Germany that had survived the fire, plus gilded
walnuts, cranberry strings, and other homemade pretties. Under
the tree was a miniature barnyard with animals and buildings of
all kinds and a tiny white fence all the way around the base of the

The new Victrola on Christmas morning at The Ranch, about 1928.

tree. While Grandma, Momma, and Aunt Grace bustled around in the kitchen and dining room, the men sat in the living room and argued politics and we six grandchildren either played games or wandered between the kitchen and the Christmas tree.

And finally, dinner. What a vision that table was. You hardly dared touch anything, it was so elegant—the Haviland china, sparkling crystal water glasses, the whitest of linen tablecloths—Grandma set a table fit for a king. What was served for dinner I can't remember, other than the turkey, which Grandpa carved with the expertise of a French chef, and the dessert, which was always ice cream and sunshine cake.

"A-a-a-h," Grandpa would sigh contentedly as he cleaned up the last drop of ice cream. "If I could choose the way to die, I'd like to be buried under a mountain of ice cream and die while I was eating my way out."

The first Christmas I spent away from Crawford proved to me the strength of home ties. I was a freshman in college at Boulder, Colorado, with very little money—certainly not enough to make the trip home across the mountains. As the first snows came and the days shortened, I began to realize that I was actually going to be homesick. And then, the week before Christmas, a package arrived. It was a large box, so large it took two of us to get it to my room. All the girls gathered round, wanting me to open it.

"Was it heavy?" No, it wasn't.

"Maybe it's some new clothes." I knew better.

"May we see?" I didn't see why not.

But I wasn't prepared for what we did see. First came the fragrance of warm cedar. Then I saw green branches. And as I lifted the contents out, we all stood stunned. There on the table was a miniature Christmas tree, a *real* one, decorated with bits of bright yarn, tiny balls, and real gilded walnuts. Instructions in Grandpa's careful handwriting told me that the walnuts were to be opened Christmas morning—and when I did, I found a dollar bill tucked in each shell. There were twenty of them—or in today's currency at least a hundred dollars. Quite a gift! Actually, though, the money simply got spent, but the memory has remained an everlasting present.

9. Work and Play

IN THE bottom drawer of my dresser is a set of seven dish towels that I have kept for years but hesitate to use. I keep them as a memento of days long gone. Few people dry dishes anymore, and those who do probably never use such towels as these. They were made of bleached flour sacks and embroidered with illustrations of each day's job:

> Monday—Wash Day
> Tuesday—Ironing
> Wednesday—Mending
> Thursday—Market Day
> Friday—Baking
> Saturday—Cleaning
> Sunday—Church

We followed this regimen religiously. On Monday we did the washing—everything from aprons to overalls. That evening we sorted the tubs of clean sun-dried clothes into groups for Tuesday's ironing. Some needed to be starched and some "sprinkled," and all were rolled in towels or sheets to keep them damp overnight. Next day we ironed all the clothes, including the sheets, towels, and underwear.

The week continued as outlined on the towels through mending, marketing, baking, and cleaning. During the summer months many other chores were added to the routine: watering the yard and garden, weeding, hoeing, picking vegetables. Finally there was canning, a job that makes me tired just to think about.

Some people enjoy canning. I don't like it now and I positively hated it then. The buckets of peas to shell or beans to snap seemed endless. When we canned fruit, everything got sticky with sugar or honey syrup. The kitchen was always hot and steamy. Lids and jars had to be sterilized, and the big canner had to be kept boiling to seal the jars of food.

It was exhausting, dirty work. But I know we felt proud when twenty pints of little green peas or thirty quarts of peaches sat in shining rows on the back porch table, waiting to be taken "down cellar."

Many of these special jobs were a joint effort between us and the Drexel grandparents across the street. I have no idea who was boss of this working federation, although I doubt it was Momma. Grandma didn't take orders very well.

Although those seven dish towels didn't mention doing dishes, this was, of course, a thrice-daily job—one that no one liked and that we three girls tried to get out of whenever we could. To this day, my sister Rie accuses me of always "needing" to practice the piano just at dish-washing time. She's probably right!

People don't do dishes anymore, at least not in the sense I mean. I know that everyone has dirty dishes that must be cleaned in some fashion, mostly with dishwashers these days. But washing dishes the way we did it is nearly a lost art. Maybe it was just a Den Beste habit, or the western way, or perhaps it was a Dutch custom—I don't know. All I know is that we Did the Dishes, with capital D's.

Our kitchen table was built against the wall under the south windows. It had a shelf underneath and the top was covered in zinc. Two dishpans, each about twenty-five inches across, resided on the shelf, ready to set up on the table side by side.

First we brought in the dishes from the dining room and scraped the crumbs off the tablecloth with a silver crumb scraper or a table knife. Sometimes Momma did the "crumbing" even before she got up from the table—at least as far as she could reach. It became an unconscious habit of hers, in fact.

Next we filled the big teakettle and made *boiling* water on the stove. While that was heating, we scraped the dirty dishes, rinsed them in the sink, and stacked them neatly behind the pans. Our sink hung beside the table, had one big shallow bowl, and only a cold-water faucet. Next we filled the left-hand dishpan with cold water and some of the boiling water. Then came the soapsuds, which we made by using a small wire cage on a long handle that was filled with old pieces of soap. We swished this contraption around in the warm water. Washing was done in steps: glasses first, next silverware, then china. Each piece was washed in the left-hand pan, rinsed in boiling water in the right-hand pan, dried immediately, then put away.

The pots and pans came last, of course. If we hadn't done the scraping right, by this time we'd have to start over with new boiling water, soapsuds—the whole bit. But an experienced dishwasher could manage with the original pans of water.

Last but not least, the dishpans must be dried and put on their shelf, the towels hung up neatly, and the zinc table scoured. This was Doing the Dishes as I learned it.

But no matter how busy everyone was most days, there was always time for fun and relaxation. Grandma saw to that! Like the August day when I was eleven and Grandma decided to play hooky from work. She vowed she'd had enough of canning and cleaning. In fact, she declared, this would be a fine day to take the older grandchildren swimming.

Well! That would be quite an adventure for us, because the nearest swimming pool was in the town of Delta, forty miles away. All the better, as far as Grandma was concerned—it would mean a whole day free from work.

We left Crawford in a cloud of dust, with Grandma driving faster than the law allowed. All the way to Delta we sang silly songs like:

> It ain't gonna rain no more, no more,
> It ain't gonna rain no more;
> How in the heck can I wash my neck
> If it ain't gonna rain no more?

When we tired of singing, we watched for Burma Shave signs. We were about halfway to Delta when we spotted the familiar row of red and white signs. These read: "His Face Was Smooth/And Cool As Ice/And Oh Louise!/He Smelled/So Nice/Burma Shave." There were always six signs, set just far enough apart that one could read them at thirty to thirty-five miles per hour. When Daddy or

Momma drove we had no trouble, but Grandma tended to speed, so we had to be alert. The real challenge was to read the signs on the left as you passed them. It's hard to remember a poem backwards, like: "Burma Shave/Fifth Divorce/Caused His/And That's What/Was Stiff And Coarse/Grandpa's Beard."

When we got to the swimming pool we were more than ready to get into that cool-looking water. But first we had to rent bathing suits because we didn't own any.

"Grandma, do we have to get these black ones?" Mary Edith groaned.

"I don't see any other color available, I'm afraid. Don't worry, honey, they will be fine. Now go to the dressing rooms and change. I have to do some errands and will be back in about an hour." And with that, Grandma left us to fend for ourselves.

Ralph, who had always been a daredevil, took one look at that fine pool and leaped in. He had played in Crawford's swimming hole behind the flour mill for nearly all of his ten years, but it wasn't deep, like this pool. That didn't seem to worry Ralph any. He took off, dog-paddling for the deep end.

Mary Edith may have felt embarrassed in her rented black-wool suit, which resembled a long-legged leotard cut off just above the knees, but she solved that easily enough. She simply put on her acting airs. She walked along the side of the pool with her movie-star walk, swinging her hips and holding her head high. She pretended to be twenty-one instead of twelve, just the way she did at home sometimes.

As for me—I felt completely miserable. How could I go out there in that ugly black thing? If only I could snap my fingers and disappear. The water looked so deep it frightened me. I couldn't swim, and I couldn't just stand there, so I carefully climbed down into the pool and stayed to myself in one corner, waiting for the hour to pass. While I waited I made a decision: I would learn to act grown-up like Mary Edith and someday I would earn enough money to buy a beautiful bathing suit.

For days after that I practiced walking and swinging my hips and laughing prettily at imaginary people. I even practiced winking. But it was a long time before I dared try my new skills in the open, and much longer still before the bathing suit became a reality.

My sisters and me on the fence in front of our house. From left: *Katy, Rie, Myrtle.*

Eleven is a between-time age, it seems to me. I remember the strange feelings that stirred in me when I practiced winking and thought of a certain dark-haired boy. Yet I also remember how childishly I cried in fear one day that same summer.

It was late in August, just before school started. Rie and I, looking for something to do, decided to clean the playhouse. We scrubbed and polished everything, sorted through the summer's collection of rocks and arrowheads, washed the dolls' blankets, and got everything shipshape for fall and winter. Then we decided to spend the night there as a sort of farewell party. Three blankets from Momma's closet made a fine bed on the floor. We put peanut butter and honey sandwiches, apples, and oatmeal cookies in the little cupboard and felt all ready for our night out.

The playhouse had been built in a gully just west of our house. Between the playhouse and the street Momma and Daddy had terraced the sides of the gully with rocks to form flower beds, and they had planted a lawn in the center. It was as perfect as a picture, at least in our eyes, and especially now that the little house was orderly and clean.

We ate our supper and washed the little tin dishes and put the dolls to bed. But just as we settled down on the blankets to play

My parents, my sisters, and me. The Jitney is behind us.

"Authors," the wind started to blow and the sky turned dark. Thunder began to roll down from the mountains.

Even though I was used to thunder and lightning and thought I had conquered my early terror of both, there was something odd about this storm. I felt as if we were in a strange, magnetized place—an unexplainable sensation—and then it was that I felt the hot wash of real fear.

Flash after flash of lightning lit up the sky. The thunder was so loud it seemed as though Zeus and Thor and everyone else up there must be having a whale of a fight. Suddenly an explosion of sound and light burst all around us. The playhouse seemed to be bathed in fire, alive and trembling. Rie started to cry, but I was so terror-stricken that I just stared out the window as our whole universe became a gray mass of water pouring down from the sky. A moment later I noticed a trickle of water coming in under the front door and, looking out at the front lawn, I realized that the gully was now a sea of water that was level with the floor of the playhouse porch. I began to cry too—we were in a real flood.

And then the door opened and there stood Daddy in his big hip boots and rubber raincoat! He scooped up Rie and two blankets and ran for the house. In a minute he was back for me and the other blanket, leaving the playhouse to the mercy of the storm.

That cloudburst did a lot more than frighten two little girls and flood a playhouse. Almost every yard in town was covered with a layer of mud and rocks that the water had carried down from Young's Peak. Cellars became pools of dirty water, the streets were full of debris, lawns and flower beds were completely ruined. When the mud finally dried it turned to gray dust, which remained to plague housewives for weeks and weeks. Our clean playhouse was a mess, and school started before we could repair all the damage.

I learned more than one lesson that day. I realized that although human beings often think they are masters of this world, it isn't so. We're all midgets compared to mighty Nature.

The other lesson is something I couldn't have expressed then. Only now do I begin to understand. If there is a God who is more powerful than Nature, then His essence is Love. And He shows Himself through people. It was Daddy who waded through the storm to save Rie and me because he loved us. As Paul said, "and now abideth faith, hope, love, these three; but the greatest of these is love."

10. Grade-School Adventures

FIFTH GRADE! Oh, how adult it seemed to finally reach that exalted spot. Finally we were upstairs at school. Here we played with all the big kids and looked with disdain on those babies down there on the basement level. We could hear the high-school bell for changing classes and we had recess with the seventh- and eighth-graders. Boy, did we feel grown up!

The other good thing about fifth grade was that my Aunt Edith, one of Earl's older sisters, was our teacher. She wanted us to call her "Miss Edith," but every time Earl and I tried to call her that we got the giggles; so she finally pretended not to notice when she became "Aunt Edith" or just "Edith."

But the road to growing up had pitfalls, and one of mine concerned a seventh-grade girl who didn't like me. Her name was Darlene Richy and she called me things like "Dirty Myrt" and "Little Miss Long-nose." I had always disliked my long, pointed, prominent nose. It seemed to me that I had inherited both my grandfathers' noses. And I hated being teased about it.

Recess was the worst time, of course, but I soon discovered that a few of the girls played marbles with the boys rather than jumped rope with the girls. I joined the marbles game and in just a little while I developed some real skill. We each carried our own favorite

78

The Crawford schoolhouse, which combined grade school and high school, as I knew it. Young's Peak rises behind.

steelies and agates to school in small drawstring bags, sometimes playing for keeps in order to take possession of another's prize taw.

In early October, Darlene had a birthday party and invited all the town girls except me. After suffering silently for a few days, I thought of a way to get even. I challenged Darlene to a game of marbles—for keeps. And I did it in front of everybody at recess, so she didn't dare refuse. We set the game for the next day during afternoon recess.

Well, the game went just as I'd planned. I demolished Darlene. When the bell rang she had only six marbles left, and my bag was full to overflowing. I went home that afternoon in a rosy glow. But I hadn't counted on Daddy's reaction.

"Do you mean to tell me you've been gambling at marbles?" he demanded.

"Well, I won fair and square!" I countered.

"No daughter of mine is going to do any gambling as long as I know anything about it," declared Daddy. "Now you just take those marbles back down to Darlene right now. You'll have time before supper."

I was aghast. But there was no use in arguing with him: He didn't seem interested in my reasons. To him it was all very simple: I had done wrong and I had to make it right.

So I took the marbles down to Darlene's house. But I didn't give them to her—I just quietly opened the screen door to the front porch, put the marbles on the floor, and sneaked away. After that, there was an uneasy truce between us. We weren't friends, but at least she stopped teasing me.

Just before Halloween that year we added one more member to our family: a scrawny, gray half-grown kitten. It was Rie who found Muggsie and brought her home.

"Please, Momma, can we keep her? She's purring so loud! I don't think she has anybody to love her and take care of her. Please?" Rie put her whole soul into her plea.

"I'm afraid"—but Momma wasn't really sure what she was afraid of; only that she didn't like cats very well and didn't want the responsibility for this one.

Rie's eyes started to brim over with tears. "I'll take care of her all the time, Momma. I'll feed her every day and brush her hair, and I won't ever let her get on your bed."

"Well-l-l—" Momma hesitated. Finally she said it was all right to let her stay outside, and Rie could fix a bed for her down in the cellar.

Nothing could have pleased Rie more. She was really in her element when she was nursing some little hurt or helpless critter. She had such a firm but gentle touch; such a quiet, reassuring voice; such a way with all frightened animals. Rie has always been this way, with animals and people, and seems to have been born a nurse. She seems to know instinctively just how to comfort and reassure.

Little Muggsie did her best to obey the rules, and submitted happily to all the love and attention. As she grew stronger and more secure, it became evident that she was also a pretty smart cat and willing to earn her keep. Mice, snakes, and moles were brought to the porch door for inspection and approval before she carted them off again for a leisurely feast. Sometimes she asked to come in for an afternoon nap, but she carefully chose the leather couch in the living room and never once tried to hop up on a bed. Slowly but surely she won over Momma's affection until the time came when Momma would fix her an extra bit of bread and milk for supper.

Katy and Muggsie at Grandma Drexel's house.

We had had cats around the yard before, but never one like Muggsie. She was a very independent creature and could take care of herself with no help from us. But she also seemed to understand when someone needed a friend, and at those times stayed close to rub and purr companionably. Muggs remained an integral member of the family long after we three girls left home. In fact, she and Grandpa became such friends that she eventually moved across the street and let him pamper her in her old age.

Cats and cows and chickens are all very helpful in the sex education of children, but even so, there are lots of unanswered questions to be faced by embarrassed parents. Even though we had helped Muggsie bring her first kittens into the world, had seen Susie give birth to at least one of her calves, and had even seen the borrowed bull chase and mount our cow more than once, still we wondered about babies. Momma was much too inhibited to talk about such things, so it fell to Daddy to supply the answers. He solved the problem by giving me a book for my birthday entitled *Being Born*. It had all the necessary pictures and carefully worded text, which I studied in the privacy of my room. Then I let Earl borrow the book. So by the spring of our fifth-grade year we knew not only fractions and the geography of Asia and the story of *David Copper-field,* but we knew how babies were made, too. We felt educated!

Our new knowledge also got us into trouble. It happened at the last-day-of-school picnic. The fifth-and-sixth-grade room decided to go to Needle Rock for its picnic that year, and Aunt Edith persuaded one of the school bus drivers to take us.

Needle Rock makes you catch your breath, it's such an unexpected sight. Taller than most city skyscrapers and as big around as several city blocks, it sits high in the valley of the Smith Fork Creek near the base of Saddle Mountain and seems to guard the whole valley like a medieval castle. The name is not very apt, though. It really looks more like a giant mitten. I'm told that in earlier years there was a hole in the rock that resembled the eye of a needle, and perhaps there was.

The school bus got us to Needle Rock about 11:00 A.M., and as soon as we got everything unpacked we ate all the goodies we'd brought from home. Then we were free to climb and explore for an hour, when it was time to meet at the bus again.

Most of the kids took off straight up the hill toward the base of the rock, but Earl noticed one boy and girl, who had been sweethearts for the last two weeks, heading off to the west alone.

"Oh-oh," he said to me, "we shouldn't let them go off alone. They might get into *trouble!*" And he rolled his eyes knowingly.

I agreed wholeheartedly. After all, knowing what we knew, we felt responsible for at least trying to stop them. I can't imagine now how I could have thought anyone would want to make love on that steep hillside covered in cactus, sagebrush, and rocks, but I did. Such innocence!

Well, we took off after those kids. The trouble was that we never did find them, but in the process of looking we became lost. We hiked and climbed until we found ourselves hopelessly tangled in a thicket of oak brush. Then we had to hunt and pick our way out of that, scramble under a barbed-wire fence, and wade across a small irrigation ditch. We finally arrived back at the picnic site, completely bedraggled, only to find the bus and all the kids gone!

We just sat down by the side of the road, too tired to care much about anything. By the time the bus came back for us I realized

Needle Rock. Photograph by Petley Studios, Phoenix, Arizona.

we were in trouble. We'd most likely have to go to the school office for a whipping, and I'd probably get a spanking from Daddy, too.

The bus driver did take us directly to the school office, where Mr. Gorsuch was waiting. But for some reason he didn't spank us after all. Maybe we looked so beat and subdued that he decided we had suffered enough already.

Daddy didn't spank me either. After I'd explained what happened and why we did it, he got a funny look on his face, as if he might be about to choke or something, turned away for a minute, and then told me to go clean up for supper. The subject was never mentioned again.

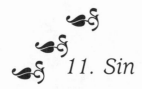

11. Sin

WHEN I was eight I joined the WCTU (Women's Christian Temperance Union) and took The Pledge. Meetings were held every other week in the Sunday School room of the church annex. We went after school and met for about forty-five minutes, listening to first one mother, then another tell us of the evils of strong drink. The preacher told us how sinful it was, and a guest speaker from Delta showed us how you could cook egg white in alcohol. That was strong stuff! It would be unthinkable to drink anything that could cook your insides like that. So, naturally, I pledged myself to Total Abstinence. And within a year I had sinned grievously. Without even realizing it, I broke my pledge and doomed myself to hell.

It all happened when I spent the night with Helen Bailey. She lived out on Piburn Flats, so I got to ride the bus home with her.

Momma had told me how to be a good guest, how I must help with the dishes and make my bed and eat whatever was served, even if I didn't like it. I was a finicky eater but I promised to do my best.

We had a good time playing together, and supper turned out all right too, although Mrs. Bailey wasn't as good a cook as Momma. But after supper Mr. Bailey brought something up from the cellar in a big jug. It was a foamy dark brown drink and he poured a glass full for each of us. I tried and tried to drink it but I could only manage three swallows or so. It tasted *awful.*

Next day I told the family all about it. "The only bad thing was a drink Mr. Bailey called 'home brew.' I only managed part of that. But I really did try, Momma."

Momma's face turned white and she said, "Oh my! Myrtle you've broken your pledge. That was *beer* you drank."

"But I thought beer was called 'three-point-two.' Honest, I didn't know."

"That doesn't make any difference. You broke a promise and that's a sin."

"Now Esther, it's not as bad as all that," said Daddy. "I expect God will forgive her this time . . ." And he gave me a little hug to show that at least *he* had forgiven me already.

Having fallen from grace by the age of nine, I began to see things around me with new eyes, as though a curtain of velvet had suddenly been replaced with one of gauze. Things I hadn't understood before began to make sense.

I was shocked at first to realize that everybody sins now and then. But I understood now why Ezra Dowdy, who lived somewhere below Crawford, could go around carousing, drunk as a hoot owl, on Saturday night and then come to Wednesday night prayer meeting and give testimony about being a Christian. When Ferris Edwards stole his boss's hunting rifle he could be forgiven, just as Daddy said I was. At least he could if he said he was sorry and didn't steal again.

Of course, when Homer Willis stole his cousin's wife—well, that was a sin that everyone agreed was going to be hard for the Lord to forgive. I didn't see how Homer could ever pray his way out of that.

Anyway, now that I understood a little better about sin and forgiveness and which things are honestly sinful and what things are just someone else's idea of wrong, I began to try my wings a little. I wore shorts to the drugstore one day and didn't feel bad about it at all. I wondered why shorts were considered off limits. I told my friend Helen a small lie and knew instantly that I had sinned. By the time I reached eighth grade I had begun to possess a fairly good understanding of right and wrong.

Then dancing came into the picture. Gramma and Grampa Den Beste said it was sinful, just like smoking and card-playing.

Momma thought so too, although she was less vehement. Daddy said he couldn't see any reason for dancing to be classed as a sin.

"It's because it lets the boys and girls get too close to each other," said Momma, blushing as she said it.

"Well, so does hugging. And I sure don't think it's sinful to hug you good," replied Daddy with a big wink to me.

"That's different!" But Momma knew she had lost the argument.

I was glad of that, because I wanted to join the dancing classes that had recently been instituted by Mr. Mulay, the new school principal. He was also the coach, teaching softball in the fall, basketball in the winter, and track in the spring. For sports, the girls practiced under his direction on Mondays and Wednesdays and the boys did their practicing on Tuesdays and Thursdays. On Friday Mr. Mulay required all of us to go out to the gym and dance. A student had to have a note from home to get out of it. He put a jukebox in the corner below the stage and provided as many records as the school budget would allow. Then he and the three other high school teachers tried to teach all forty of us to dance. Most of us learned a few steps and everyone was introduced to the etiquette required of young ladies and gentlemen.

From that beginning it was an easy step to go to a real dance. My first dancing date was for the Junior-Senior Prom, held in the same gym where we learned to dance. It didn't seem frightening at all. It was, in fact, a lot of fun. Most of the community was there, all dressed to the teeth and ready to live it up. The music was a live band called The Fobare Family. They had a fiddle, guitar, piano, banjo, and sax. I think there was a bass fiddle too. They played for all the dances in the area.

By the time I was in high school, Momma had relaxed her fears about dancing. She might not have been so complacent, however, if she had known about The Bucket of Blood. I went there only once—on a dare—and knew I'd never go again. It was a dance hall way out in the country by itself. My escort assured me it was safe enough, but I wasn't so sure—I'd heard so many rumors. There were six or seven unsavory characters hanging around outside, pulling on whiskey bottles. Inside it was noisy and smoky. Some of the dancers, already drunk, stumbled around in everybody's way. We stayed for a dance or two, then left, grateful not to have been hit over the head with a beer bottle. But I could say I'd been there!

I was grateful to Mr. Mulay for including social dancing in the curriculum. Was there another high school that did such a thing? Perhaps we were unique in that respect.

Our high school was unusual in other ways, too. It could afford only four teachers, yet it offered sixteen basic courses: those needed for college eligibility as well as band, typing, and the sports program. The students also gave plays, held proms, had cheerleaders, and went on class trips. How in the world did those teachers manage such a schedule? But of course each class was small. Ours had a total of nine members, and the class of '42, the one before us, had four graduates.

We were lucky, I think, in being a small school that offered so much. Some of our teachers were very good teachers, too. One I remember particularly was Miss Keihmyer. Actually, I disliked her, just as everyone else did. But I recognized that she was teaching me a lot.

Miss Keihmyer was a flamboyant person with a love of the dramatic and a flair for being different. She wore wildly printed scarves over her blouses, always knotted in some unconventional way. A cape was more her style than a sweater or jacket. She always wore high heels, which were not very practical in our graveled-path world. But her specialty was sneezes: she had a complete repertoire. One went *Wh-o-o-sh*. Another was the traditional *Ah-ah-ah-choo!* There was one that ended with a question mark and one that seemed to go on and on indefinitely. But none of them was quiet. Her sneezes could be heard in every room of the school, upstairs and down.

Miss Keihmyer taught English and Latin, and she tended to specialize in the grammar of both subjects. Declensions, conjugations, the diagramming of sentences—all were dealt with at length. Every day it was, "Write out *all* the forms of 'to go,' in all tenses, both active and passive." Every day we sang out "present tense, past tense, future tense"—and on and on.

Earl, who was especially bright, soon tired of the whole thing. He learned to sleep through most of the class, waking up just long enough to recite when his turn came. But one day he failed to wake up in time. Miss Keihmyer stared for a moment, then got up and stomped over to his seat. Grabbing the sleeping victim's hair, she pulled him upright and yelled in her most penetrating voice, "You! You imbecile! You are the epitome of stupidity!" Earl's eyes bugged way out and the room was suddenly so quiet you could have heard a feather fall.

I've often wondered if Earl knew what "epitome" meant, or if, like me, he went straight to the dictionary when he got home. I added several words to my vocabulary that year, words like "pique" and "irrelevant," "unique," "germane," and "umbrage," all presented in context.

Miss Keihmyer didn't stay in Crawford very long—three years or so, I think. She probably didn't like any of us any better than we liked her. She needed a larger theater, and such things as the WCTU simply filled her with loathing. But I'm glad she was there to teach me the drama of words.

12. Changes and Nostalgia

IN 1936 the Drexel grandparents had a visit from Uncle Guy, who lived in New York. He wasn't really related—that was just the grown-ups' way of speaking about him to us children. Back in the days when Daddy had been in college, he had persuaded one of his class-mates to spend the summer working with him in the bee yards at home. Guy, who was a city fellow, had enjoyed the work and the family so much that he had spent several more summers working for Grandpa, and he remained a firm friend of the family the rest of his life. In 1936 he was a chemist working for Lederle Labora-tories. Uncle Guy had recently gone on a business trip to California, and he had some very exciting news about his trip there. After dinner at Grandpa's he told us about it as we all sat in the living room.

I listened in disbelief as Uncle Guy told how he had seen a thing called a cyclotron that could split an atom. How could that be? I had just learned at school that the atom was the smallest particle of matter in the universe. How could anything be smaller than that? Questions tumbled around in my mind. Was the schoolbook wrong? What would half an atom be called? Could half an atom be cut in half too? I didn't understand any of it, but I did realize that I was hearing something important.

The conversation ranged over many things, such as new ways to extract vitamins and put them in pills for people to take, and new

89

inventions such as the automatic dishwasher. A dishwasher? I instantly envisioned a sort of mechanical man who, at the press of a button, would gather up all the dishes, then wash and dry them and put them away.

Finally Grandpa said, "You know, the way things are going, I believe someday we'll even get a man to the moon and find out it's not made of green cheese after all." We all laughed, but something in the way he said it made me think he really did believe men would make such a journey someday.

So many changes! One had just recently happened at our house. We had a brand new Frigidaire, a marvelous invention that kept things cold without having to have a block of ice put in it. And it even made its own ice in little cubes that were just the right size to fit in iced tea glasses.

Up until now we had gotten ice from a pond in wintertime and stored it for summer use in the icehouse that stood next to the coal and wood sheds. I remember the excitement of watching the men lift the big blocks of ice from a wagon onto a wide board and slide them into the icehouse. They packed snow down into the cracks between the blocks and over each layer of ice. Finally, a blanket of sawdust was laid all around the walls and on top of the ice for insulation. There the ice stayed until it was needed, all the way through summer and fall. Now the icehouse was no longer used at all. It was just an empty old building.

Electricity was, in fact, changing our lives in many ways. We now had an electric iron, which replaced a much bigger and clumsier thing that burned coal oil. I suppose this oil-burning iron was thought to be an improvement over the heavy flatirons that we had heated on the stove surface. These had either hot iron handles or a removable wooden one, which could be changed from iron to iron. I, for one, preferred them to the newer oil iron because it was *very* heavy, and hot and smelly besides. It had a small tank, where the coal oil was burned, in front of the iron and the handle. I always felt it might blow up at any minute, which, of course, it never did. When we finally got a brand new electric iron, I was ecstatic. This was real progress!

A few families in Crawford got new electric stoves, but the black coal range continued to serve our family until long after I left home in the forties. It cooked the meals, warmed the kitchen, and heated the water in the bathroom tank. Talk about hot water—sometimes turning on the bathtub tap was a dangerous act! When the stove had been used for baking, the water seemed almost like steam, having just passed through coils along the side of the fire box in a stove that had been kept at 350 degrees for over an hour.

Another piece of equipment of that day was a separator for efficiently separating cream from milk. I don't know how many ranchers or farmers used separators, only that *we* had one in the cellar and used it every evening. Daddy did the job as soon as he finished milking Suzy. He poured the milk into a large, shiny metal bowl that had two spouts coming out near the bottom. The spouts, one a little higher than the other, emptied into two smaller bowls, one for cream and one for skim milk. The separating part was a chamber in the bottom half of the big bowl. This compartment held a circular series of thin, curved metal leaves, which were attached at the center. This whole piece could be made to whirl around and around with some speed by a series of gears and a handle.

I have wondered since why Daddy bothered with the separator, when it would have been possible to simply leave the milk in pans, allow the cream to rise to the top, and skim it off. Of course, that takes several hours, and leaving fresh warm milk without refrigeration or cooling invites bacteria. Probably it was safer to separate it and get it cooled quickly. The separator was a pain in the neck to wash because each metal leaf (they seemed to number hundreds) had to be cleaned separately. All three of us girls tried to find reasons for not doing the supper dishes because of the separator.

Each new invention and development is designed to save work or time, and I'm sure they really do. But the modern telephone system lacks the heart and soul of the local co-op phone company that I grew up with. I could turn the crank on the wall phone, lift the receiver, and when Central said "Number please," all I had to do was say "19-I" or just "Aunt Grace, please." Central knew my voice without being told and knew who my Aunt Grace was, too. In fact, "Central" was probably the best-informed person in the whole community. She knew who was sick, where everyone's children were, and how to find the doctor. She could also be counted on to act fast in any emergency. Crawford had no fire department.

Crawford's main street in about 1923. From left: bank, grocery store, cheese factory, schoolhouse (in background), the dry-goods and drugstore, telephone office, garage.

Instead, we simply called Central, and she immediately activated every plug on the switchboard to get the word out. It took only minutes to gather a crew.

There were three operators and they worked an eight-hour day shift, a four-hour evening shift, or a twelve-hour nighttime shift. The little building that housed the office and the bedroom for the night operator was neat and tidy, painted white, and kept spotless. It contained a small stove that not only heated the two little rooms but served as a warming surface for water and soup. The bathroom was the old-fashioned "two-holer" out back. Wages started at ten cents an hour in 1920, but by the thirties the amount was at least twice that.

Aunt Agnes (she was not my aunt, but was "Aunt Agnes" to everyone) and Nellie Dodge were the two operators I remember best. When there was nothing else to do, it was interesting to go up to the telephone office and watch Central plugging and unplugging the wires. Sometimes the board looked like a whole bunch of snakes mixed together with their heads stuck in metal holes.

Most rural areas of that day had similar small local telephone services. Ours eventually joined with nearby towns and communities to form the Delta County Co-operative Telephone Company, which, I think, is still an active company. Grandpa served on the board of directors from the beginning, and Daddy continued the Drexel presence on the board into the 1970s.

Long-distance connection to the Bell Telephone System was, on the other hand, an entirely different matter. There were only two Bell phones in town—one at the telephone office and one at the drugstore. If you wanted to make a long-distance call you had to go downtown to one of those phones. And, of course, when someone received a call, he had to go to one of those places to take it. It's easy to see why "long distance" was almost synonymous with "emergency." Eventually Mr. Savage had a private Bell phone installed in his office at the bank, and other businesses followed suit. The ordinary householder, however, simply didn't use long distance unless it was truly necessary.

Two other memories make me very glad we now have so many conveniences. One is the recollection of what it took to wash clothes in those days.

We didn't have a washing machine, but Grandma Drexel had a good electric one—at least the washing part was electric—the wringer worked manually. So Monday's washing became a joint project. Momma sorted our clothes and we helped her cart them across the street. Grandpa had the washing machine and two rinse tubs all set up in the middle of the kitchen floor with hoses attached to the sink faucets. It was all arranged so the wringer at the edge of the washing machine could swing across the rinse tubs, one containing bluing and the other a final rinse. Washing went on all morning, from the white linens to the dark, dirty work overalls that had been soaking all night in another tub on the back porch. It took a long time to remove beeswax and propolis (a substance bees take from trees and use as cement in their hives).

One person put the clothes through the wringer, another sorted them into piles to carry outside. Grandpa had clotheslines strung all over the backyard, and he usually did the hanging.

In the afternoon we all helped take in the clothes. We divided them and took ours back home. That evening we sorted, folded, put things away, and dampened the clothes for Tuesday's ironing.

Most women in that day washed this way, although many had to do the job alone. And many had gasoline-powered machines, rather than the electric machine Grandma Drexel had. I'm grateful that job has gone with the horse and buggy. I do not mourn the demise of the old washing machine.

One more word about washing: Consider handkerchiefs. There was no Kleenex in those days. We boiled our hankies each week and hung them separately. Like everyone else, my family used both the Sunday linen kind and everyday rags that were cut from old dish towels and sheets. I, for one, hope we can keep boxed tissues around forever.

One other memory involves carrots, potatoes, and crickets. It was like a nightmare. It went like this:

Momma: Myrtle, go down cellar and get me eight good carrots.

Myrtle: Oh, please Momma, do I *have* to?

Daddy: Come on, 'fraidy cat, don't be silly. You're a big girl now.

Nothing for it but to go down cellar, go to the big wooden box where the carrots and potatoes were stored, lift the lid, and locate all the crickets.

Crickets! I've never liked them very much, although we had one, a little black musician, who lived under the table leg and sang every night while we studied. Black ones weren't so bad, but those in the box were white. They lived in the dark potato-carrot box all their lives and had no color at all. Little jumping, pale, ghostly crickets!

So I had to locate a good carrot, close my eyes, reach in, and pray nothing would leap at me. Eight times I had to hope and reach while my heart raced and my mouth went dry.

I'm glad I can now go to a beautiful grocery store and pick up carrots and potatoes, fresh and clean, from well-lit bins. Hooray for progress!

13. People and Stories

ONE GLOOMY winter Sunday the Den Bestes came to our house for dinner. I can't recall now just who was included—probably the grandparents and Earl and Lester. I do remember some of what we had to eat: smoked ham, which I hated; riced potatoes, which reminded me of worms; and watermelon pickles, which I liked better than ice cream.

After dinner and dishes we lounged contentedly in the living room and talked about this and that. The subject of people's relatives came up and launched a discussion of who was related to whom in Crawford. We finally agreed that everyone could claim kin in the area except Mr. and Mrs. Elkins. We couldn't figure a single relative anywhere around for them.

I didn't know much about the Elkins family, although I had known them all my life. Mrs. Elkins was a large, imposing woman who took charge wherever she was. You might say she was bossy. Mr. Elkins was a Caspar Milquetoast kind of man. He was stooped— probably from arthritis—and walked with a slow, shuffling gait, as though he didn't want to get where he was going but knew he must. His clothes hung on him unpressed and baggy, making him look like an old scarecrow.

Mr. Elkins had been a rural-route mail carrier for as long as I could remember, and probably long before that. His route went south from Crawford, then west across Fruitland Mesa, down the long, winding Anderson Grade, across the Smith Fork Creek, and back into Crawford along the edge of Smith Fork Canyon. For many years he delivered mail from a horse-and-buggy rig.

The story goes that he trained the horse to stop by itself at each mailbox without orders from him. While the horse traveled, he went to sleep. When the horse stopped, he woke up long enough to slide the mail into the box, then napped again until the next stop. When he got to the Anderson Grade he had a long, peaceful slumber while the horse negotiated the steep, twisting road alone.

The postal authorities finally made Mr. Elkins drive a truck instead of the horse and buggy, thinking to economize on time spent in travel. This worried my Uncle Bill, the postmaster for Crawford. How would Mr. Elkins stay awake long enough to drive that route? Mr. Elkins said not to worry, he'd drink lots of coffee before he started. Driving the truck didn't save any time after all, however. Old Mr. Elkins had to make so many stops to unburden himself of the coffee that he pulled into Crawford at the same time he always had.

Another person I knew very little about was Ol Lewis. His first name was Oliver, but I never heard anyone use that name. As a child, I thought he was so big that his name was "All" Lewis. He ran a grocery store down near the pool hall and specialized in fresh meat. He was tall and fat and drank beer the way most people drink water. I'd seen a picture of him dressed in a cutaway coat and top hat, but most of the time he was pretty sloppy. I'd go into his store with a small feeling of dread.

"What can I do for you today, little lady?" he'd say, putting down a big mug full of strong-smelling brew.

"Momma needs three pounds of beef. And she wants you to cut off the fat please," I'd recite from memory.

Ol would go to the cold room at the rear of the store and come back with a huge side of beef slung over his shoulder. Flicking away a couple of flies, he'd dump the meat on the butcher block, sharpen a long, slender knife, and deftly cut a big slice off one end of the beef. Then he'd carefully trim off the fat, slip a piece of greasy blubber into his mouth, and chew thoughtfully as he wrapped the meat in brown paper. The odor of the raw meat combined with that of his sweaty body and the ever-present beer seemed to permeate the whole place. Trying to picture Ol as Santa Claus on Christmas Eve taxed the imagination, but I knew he played the part, and I often wondered what Ol might really be like away from the store.

When I had my choice I went to the IGA (Independent Grocers Association) store, owned by the Wilsons. Actually, Mrs. Wilson ran the store while Mr. Wilson sat by the warm potbellied stove in the middle of the room. He was totally blind, so he couldn't do much of the clerking. He spent his time chewing tobacco and practicing the art of hitting the brass spittoon, which sat on the floor about four feet from his chair. Spit—*ping!* Spit—*ping!* So it went, in a sort of rhythm interrupted only when someone came into the store. I never once saw him miss the spittoon unless it got moved from its accustomed place.

Mr. Wilson had memorized the sounds of the footsteps of many of the people who traded in the store, and he would greet them as they came in the door.

"Hello there, Myrtle Mae. How are you today," Spit—*ping!*

"I'm fine, Mr. Wilson. Can I have a can of red salmon please?" I always asked him, then he would turn and say, "Mrs. Wilson, will you find the salmon for Myrtle Mae?"

Even when I came back home for visits in later years, I could still walk into the store and unfailingly be greeted by the same "Hello there, Myrtle Mae." Spit—*ping!*

Perhaps the most colorful person in town was Robert Sutton. He was my father's age, but his mind had never grown up. He was a man-child with the mental and emotional development of an eight-year-old. His favorite toy was a cap gun that he kept in his overalls pocket. Every now and then, as he wandered the streets, he'd whip out that toy pistol, shoot an imaginary bandit, then whoop and holler in glee. It all seemed pretty strange coming from a full-grown man until you got used to it.

Someone in town helped put him to work by rigging up a big square bin on wooden runners. This was hitched to a donkey, and Robert was given the job of hauling water to local folks in town who didn't have piped water. In later years, after everyone got running water, he used his sled to haul junk to the dump. It sure was easy to hear Robert coming. Those runners grated noisily over the graveled roads while Robert shouted to the donkey and shot off his toy gun. Every now and then the poor old donkey would express his feelings with a long, loud *He-e-ha-a-ah.*

Being a junkman was something Robert took to with real enjoyment. It got so he was a walking junk heap himself. A lot of the time he wore a big overcoat with baggy pockets, and whenever some piece of junk especially appealed to him, he stuffed it into one of those pockets, which sometimes were so loaded he could hardly shuffle along with his burden.

His long-suffering mother never complained when he brought stuff home and dumped it in the yard or carried it lovingly into the house. After a few years, Robert's place was a full-fledged dump and the house a disaster. And that's the way it stayed until his mother died: Then Robert was moved to a relative's home. The house and yard were completely cleared away with a bulldozer and a dump truck, leaving no trace of former junk or habitation.

Robert spent his old age wandering around town not doing much of anything. But every Sunday he dressed up in his good suit and came to church, where he sat quietly in the last pew. After the service he would buttonhole someone and lovingly show off his prize possession, a picture of Rita Hayworth in a very tight sweater.

"See my picture?" he would say, smiling proudly. Then he'd tuck it back in his coat pocket and go home—a contented old little boy.

The mail wasn't delivered to homes in Crawford. Rather, we all went to the post office twice a day to pick it up. For those who had a minute to spare, the noon stage delivery was a favorite time to gather and talk. Fish yarns, tall tales, true stories, gossip—all this added flavor to our days.

One story concerning a dude made a big hit. It was true, too. This man, Mack somebody from Back East, was spending a couple weeks' vacation at the Hawk's Nest Dude Ranch. He asked Uncle Bill to take him out and show him how to fish a mountain stream. He'd done some river fishing, he said, but had never done any fly casting. This was music to Uncle Bill's ears—he loved to fish. No trouble a'tall, he grinned, he'd show him a good spot up the country a-ways and even lend him a rod and reel.

They left town late in the afternoon when the rainbow trout would be feeding and drove east, up past Needle Rock and on beyond Saddle Mountain. Uncle Bill found a fine beaver pond and proceeded to teach the newcomer how to cast the line into the water. It didn't take long for Mack to get the hang of it and begin to have a fine time. Even though the light was fading, neither Uncle Bill nor Mack noticed—they were busy fishing.

Mack had just thrown an exceptionally good cast, way out and arching beautifully, when something odd happened. The line didn't come down, yet it was being pulled out of the reel as fast as it could spin. Mack looked up, gasped, and shouted, "I've got something on this line but it sure as heck can't be a fish!"

"Reel it in, fella, reel it in!" cried Bill.

Mack reeled—and reeled—and there at the end of the line was a bird. The poor creature had swallowed the bait on the end of Mack's line as it flew through the air and was now struggling frantically to free itself. In the dusk the bird hadn't seen the line at all.

Uncle Bill tried over and over to pull the hook out but couldn't keep the bird quiet enough. He finally had to cut the line and watch the frenzied creature fly away in the dusk.

The two had a story all ready for the noon gossipers next day about the new species of fish called a "birdfish"—how it had both gills and wings and was so strong and fast that it swallowed the bait, broke the line, and flew away.

Another true story happened to my father. He told me about it in a letter, and he told it so well I'd like to pass it on in his own words.

"I'm a little hesitant to tell this story," he wrote. "I've told it twice and had my veracity questioned both times. It happened a few weeks ago, during our real cold weather. I wanted to talk to Robert Kraai and tried to hunt him down out in his feed lot. He wasn't there, so I walked in the tracks he'd made in the snow until I found he had crossed clear over to another lot and I got tired chasing him.

"Well, I was looking around out in that wilderness on the north rim of Smith Fork Canyon and saw what looked like a good coat out there in the snow. I went over to look. There stood a fox, so alive looking I very much hesitated to come closer. But after a minute or two I realized it couldn't be alive at all. I walked up and touched it. It was frozen solid—dead—standing up.

"At that point in my story I get asked what brand I drink nowadays! I've wished since that I had come home and got my camera to get a picture of that fox. But I didn't think at the time of having to defend my honesty. I knew I wouldn't skin a fox for its pelt, just to prove a point, even if I had a right to do it. But I could have taken a picture and I'm sure the fox would have waited.

"I told Clayton McKnight about it. 'Sure,' he said, 'that fox got into a cyanide gun. When that dust hit him in the face with his mouth wide open he was done for.' Cyanide clots the blood and, when the first clot hits the heart, the job is done—as fast as a bullet could do it. He just had time for a jump or two. His nose went down to the ground between his front paws. His antics left him standing high on his back legs and before he relaxed he froze.

"That fox was red on his under parts, gray on the sides, and darker toward the back, with an almost black stripe down his back and on his tail. I sure wish farmers would quit using cyanide and let their fellow creatures alone."

One more story floated around Crawford for a while and came to be known as "The Mosquito Myth."

Two cowhands named Chet and Scooter had a Saturday off and decided to go fishing up on Grand Mesa. They loaded up Chet's old jalopy on Friday night so they could get an early start the next day.

The road up the south side of Grand Mesa at that time was narrow, unpaved, and full of sharp hairpin curves. You couldn't go fast on it, so the trip from Crawford to the Delta cutoff and up the mountain took about two hours.

It was a fine day in early August, about as warm as it ever gets up there at that ten thousand-foot level. In fact, by the time they had parked the car down near the edge of Baron Lake, rented a rowboat from the boat house, and unloaded their gear, they were both getting sweaty. The sun really does seem close and hot up there sometimes.

Well, they rowed for a little way and got out their gear, then relaxed and took in the scenery. It was a mighty pretty place, all right: blue lake and blue sky, dark green spruce trees that reached up like hundreds of sun worshippers, rustic cabins tucked in among the trees.

The sounds were restful, too. Water lapped quietly against the shore, insects buzzed incessantly, and the wind hummed through the trees like a lullaby. The air was clear as crystal; the sun burned hot. The men lazed in the warmth a bit, then started to cast their lines. The trout cooperated splendidly. At the end of two hours, when each had half a dozen good-sized specimens, they decided to call it quits.

"You row, Chet, while I pack up the gear," said Scooter. "Let's head for the boat house."

"Okay," agreed Chet.

After a minute of steady rowing, Chet suddenly said, "What the hell—Scooter, look! What's that comin' from over to the west?"

"Gol darn! It looks like a couple 'a hawks with spears in front. Hey! They're comin' this way. They sound for all the world like mosquitoes, don't they?"

"Good Lord, I think they've seen us." Then, in a slightly panicky voice, "Hey Scooter, for God's sake, help me row!"

Scooter took one of the oars and they rowed as fast as the heavy flat-bottomed boat would go. They weren't any match for the giant mosquitoes, though. Those two monsters reached the boat when it was still twenty feet from shore.

Chet stopped rowing and used his oar like a fencer's foil. He gave one mosquito a whack on his foot-long bill. Scooter did the same, but he missed his mosquito and the critter drilled him good, right on his bare arm. He let out a howl and dove over the edge of the boat into the icy water. The boat tipped and pitched Chet into the lake too, then it capsized.

It's a good thing the men were only a few feet from shore—the lakes on Grand Mesa are too cold for swimming very far. They made it to dry land and ran as fast as their numb legs would carry them toward the truck. Jumping into the jalopy, they rolled up all the windows and just sat there, wet and shivering.

Finally Scooter looked at his arm, saw it was all bloody around the hole the mosquito had made and that it was swelling up into a baseball-sized mound.

"Hey, I gotta wrap this up somehow, Chet. I'm gonna use this bandana of yours, okay?" Then he really looked at Chet and started to laugh. "Hey, you're all wet, Chet!"

"Yeah, and you got bit by that skeeter, Scooter!" Then they both howled with laughter. They could hardly wait to get home and tell what had happened to them. But, by golly, no one would believe them.

"Oh sure, and I'll bet all those fish were three feet long too! You were probably horsing around out there and dumped yourselves."

It was disappointing to be so misunderstood, but Chet and Scooter just smiled and went around calling each other "Wet Chet" and "Skeeter Scooter."

I leave it to the reader to decide whether their tale was true or not. But before you dismiss it, you should take a trip to the top of Grand Mesa and experience the mosquitoes there for yourself. You just might become a believer in The Mosquito Myth.

14. Church

HOME, SCHOOL, and church are the institutions that hold communities together, especially small places like Crawford. I find it difficult to separate them, even in trying to describe each one alone, because they all work together, tied by bonds of common kinship and need. Even now, a visit to Crawford would be meaningless without touching base with church friends and school classmates as well as family members.

The name printed in black letters on the front window over the church door proclaimed it to be The Crawford Methodist Episcopal Church, but the reality was quite different. The Sunday School Superintendent was a Mormon; the Den Bestes, who made up a sizable portion of the congregation and a good part of the choir, were firm in their Dutch Reform beliefs; Grandma Drexel had come from a Baptist heritage and Grandpa Drexel from a German Lutheran one; and two of my best friends went to Catholic schools in Denver in the wintertime but spent summer vacation at home and took part in our church activities.

It started as a single-room sanctuary, built in 1900 from wood cut at one of the local sawmills: It was not very big, but was nicely proportioned, with a square bell tower in front that was capped by a pointed roof. By the time I was old enough to remember going to Sunday School, an annex had been built on the east side with wide

The Crawford Community Church in 1914.

folding doors that opened to the sanctuary. This addition had two rooms, one large and one small, plus an ample kitchen.

These rooms served as Sunday school on Sundays and as a community center all the rest of the time. Not everyone in Crawford went to church or took part in church activities, but everyone was familiar with the inside of the annex. Few people missed the Fall Harvest Bazaar and dinner held there. And no one who could possibly get there would think of missing the big Memorial Day dinner in May.

Memorial Day was one of the largest gatherings of the year. By ten o'clock in the morning people began arriving from all over the county, first to take baskets and vases of flowers up to the cemetery behind the church, then to gather in and around the annex for dinner and visiting. Chairs were set up in a large circle under the aging cedar tree outside the annex door. Here the men sat, smoking pipes or spitting tobacco, and talked about cattle, horses, prices, and politics. Inside, the women worked in the big kitchen, set up the long tables for serving the dinner, exchanged good news and bad, and kept an eye on one another's children.

As for the kids—it was just one big party for us. Of course, it was a little somber at the beginning, during the cemetery visit. Some people seemed so sad as they quietly set a bouquet of iris or lilacs at the base of a headstone and then stood staring off toward the mountains as if they were living in another time.

But as soon as the cemetery visit was over, it was all right for the youngsters to romp and play on the church lawn, sneak handouts from the kitchen, or slip away to the soda fountain at the drugstore down the street.

In the late afternoon, after the big dinner was all over, families began to gather for reunions, and friends who hadn't seen one another since last year found a place to visit quietly awhile.

The preacher of the Crawford church was supplied by the Colorado Conference of the Methodist Church. Part of his salary was paid by the conference and the rest by the local congregation. It was never a large salary, so we usually were sent someone who was nearly ready to retire or someone who, like Grandpa Drexel, needed to live in the clear mountain air for his health.

All the other church jobs were done by volunteers. There was no church office, no janitor, no staff of any kind. Yet all the necessary work got done. The men of the church took turns shoveling snow in winter and caring for the grass in the summer. If the roof leaked, someone quietly fixed it. If the church needed painting, everyone pitched in and painted it. The women kept the windows clean, presided over the kitchen, ran the Sunday school, and saw to the needs of shut-ins and the sick.

Sunday school came first on Sunday morning, and it started in the sanctuary with everyone meeting together for opening exercises and announcements. Then we all separated into small classes according to age. Daddy taught the teenage class, ages thirteen through eighteen or thereabouts, and met with us on the stage where the choir would later sit for church. When the class was finished, we would all help rearrange the chairs into rows next to the piano.

Most of the time we had a choir and even someone who served as choir director. And by the time I was a seventh-grader I had become the church pianist. As soon as Sunday school was over and we had dismantled the circle of chairs, I went to the annex, where the choir gathered to wait for final instructions from the preacher.

The Crawford Community Church in the 1930s.

The church bell rang, I marched back on stage to the piano and began the prelude, the preacher and choir entered solemnly and took their places, and church began.

I loved the job of church pianist. Part of the fun was the Wednesday-night choir practice. Most of the time we met at the parsonage, which was just up the street from our house. After we had practiced old and new music and chosen Sunday's selections, we would relax with a few old favorites or have fun with a trio or male quartet. Sometimes the preacher's wife made a cake or fixed popcorn and invited us into the dining room after the singing. And, if a few could be persuaded to stay for a little while, we might end up the evening with a quick game of anagrams.

The hardest part of being church pianist was finding enough interesting music for preludes, offertories, and postludes. I relied heavily on the few books of piano music I used for lessons. One day Grandpa stopped by while I was practicing and found me fussing over the problem. It seemed to me I had used everything I knew, plus arrangements of all the suitable music in the hymnal.

"Why don't you arrange one of your favorite popular tunes? I'll bet you could fix it up so no one would even recognize it. What about that thing you played for me yesterday that you liked so much?" Grandpa offered the suggestion with a completely serious face.

I considered that proposal thoughtfully. Use "Blueberry Hill" as an offertory? What a crazy idea. Still, it would be fun to try.

"You won't tell on me if I do, will you?"

"Of course not. It will be our little secret," said Grandpa as he handed Momma the mail he had brought from the post office.

I sat at the piano for a long time, playing around with that hit tune until finally I found a way to make it sound quiet and worshipful. By Sunday I had memorized the whole thing and could hardly wait to try it out.

The first part of the church service seemed to go more swiftly than usual that morning. I found myself just a bit nervous as I started the offertory. This experiment might be a total failure. I breathed a sigh of relief as the offering was brought to the front and we sang "Glory Be To The Father." Then I stole a look at Grandpa in his pew near the front. He gazed back at me without a hint of a smile and winked. It was all I could do to keep from giggling.

After church, as everyone stood outside chatting in the bright sunshine, several ladies commented on the music.

"It seemed so familiar," admitted Martha Savage, "and yet I just couldn't place it."

"Blueberry Hill," Earl whispered in my ear. "But I won't tell." And he never did.

 15. Water

THE EARLY settlers of the mountain valleys of western Colorado found a land full of contradictions: the beauty of the blue-touched mountains next to the dull brown of the arid mesas; too much water in the creeks but none for the land a few hundred yards away; fertile soil aplenty but no rain to make crops grow.

The Ute Indians had lived there for centuries, but they were not farmers. Instead, they roamed the area, following the wild game as it moved from high ground in summer to lower range areas in the cold winter months. Those people lived as nature willed, disturbed as little as possible, and left the land as they found it. The valleys and mountain meadows provided lush grass that grew waist-high. Water was easy to find, flowing in the many crystal-clear streams or gushing out of cracks and crannies along mountainsides.

When the first white settlers set foot in this paradise in the late 1800s, they saw it mostly as an opportunity to make money. Here was everything a person needed, and it was all free. Cattlemen soon brought in huge herds, moving from one grass-filled valley to another. They made no effort to conserve or replenish because there was so much more waiting to be used.

Within a decade the free ride was over. The native grass had been destroyed. Some cattlemen moved on. Others, who had fallen in love with this beautiful country, became settled ranchers and farmers. For them the need for a steady supply of water became urgent. The Crawford area's annual precipitation has always averaged less than eleven inches, and most of that comes as snow.

Those who claimed bottomland found it relatively easy to provide water for their fields by digging a ditch from the creek at some point above the land to be irrigated. But there was a great deal more fertile land far away from the creeks. Getting water to this dry ground presented problems.

Eventually farmers banded together, pooling their resources and labor, and dug large irrigation ditches from high up in the hills past their ranches and fields. They formed ditch companies and divided their water into shares. A complex list of rules governed the use of that water, from the first rush of spring water to the last trickle in the fall.

Even today the title to the water rights, meaning the amount of water that has been legally granted to a piece of property, is the first and most important consideration to a buyer of land in western Colorado.

What one man has, another man sometimes covets, especially something as precious as water. Thus, water-stealing entered the picture from the very beginning. Sometimes it was a small diversion dam above the measuring gauge, or it might be a siphon hidden under protective shrubbery. That water could spell the difference between success and disaster for a whole field of alfalfa. It became necessary for the ditch companies to hire riders to monitor the streams. And the state of Colorado hired overseers to check on the ditch companies.

Daddy became one of those overseers in about 1938. His title, I think, was Deputy Water Commissioner, and his job was to regulate the amount of water that was allowed into each ditch from the creek. In some ways it was among the best of jobs—there wasn't much hard work to do and it afforded a fine excuse for a leisurely hike up in the hills, or maybe a few minutes of contemplation beside a cool creek. But it also had its frustrations. If you got enough water in one ditch to satisfy a rancher on the high slope, then the fellow lower down would claim he was being cheated. Sometimes the headgate seemed, mysteriously, to change itself to a new setting.

"Well," said Daddy, "it takes time and a bit of tact to keep

The view from our dining room window of (left) Saddle Mountain and (right) Castle Mountain.

everybody happy. But most folks are honest enough; they know I do the best I can with the water that's available."

He was a bit less cheerful late one Saturday afternoon, though. "Ma, looks like I'm going to have to go up to the Saddle Mountain Ditch headgate tomorrow. Either somebody's stealing or there's a leak someplace."

"But that's Sunday! Can't it wait even a day?" Momma asked with a worried frown.

"Nope, afraid not. But I'll tell you what—let's take a picnic lunch and we'll all go. We can leave right after church and get back by five easily." And Daddy gave Momma a little pat on the shoulder as if to say, "Now that's all settled."

"Oh boy," shouted Katy, "maybe I can catch a fish in the creek!" And she ran off to fix up her homemade pole.

Sunday was a beautiful day with little puffy white clouds in a deep blue sky. Meadowlarks sang anthems to one another from every field. Freshly mown hay smelled deliciously sweet as it baked under the hot sun.

As we passed Needle Rock, going from sunshine to shadow beneath that towering mountain of stone, a huge bird sailed across the road in front of us. Daddy hit the brakes and the car skidded on the gravel close to the edge of the road.

"Oh my! It's an eagle!" Momma said in a reverent whisper. She was so astonished that she hadn't even noticed Daddy's rough stop.

"It sure is," agreed Daddy. "He must be hunting chipmunks or something. We almost hit him, too. You know I think his wing span must be nearly seven feet."

The eagle disappeared as suddenly as he had come, but he left an impression of great power and beauty.

When we got to the bridge over the Smith Fork Creek, Daddy parked the car in an open spot off the road, and we all piled out. Here was a grove of aspen trees, their leaves shivering in the breeze; a meadow of grass and wildflowers; and the creek, wide enough in spots to spread out and lie in quiet pools. Others had found this spot enticing, and one of the community clubs had set a picnic table and benches under a large cottonwood tree.

Momma's fried chicken, potato salad, and sour cream chocolate cake tasted even better here than at home. Sparrows and jays scolded one another and us from the branches of the nearest tree. The creek babbled happily past the picnic table. It was a lot cooler up here than in Crawford, though. I was glad Daddy had made us bring along sweaters, and I pulled mine on as Katy raced away to fish from the bridge.

For a while Rie and I sat with Momma, listening to the creek make its special music. Daddy wandered off into a thick stand of trees. Then a bee buzzed near Rie's head to investigate her shining golden hair. Rie started to hit it away when Momma cried out in a panicky voice, "Don't! Don't hit at it! Sit still until it flies away." And of course, it did just that in another moment.

"Why are you so afraid of bees, Momma?" asked Rie.

"Well, you see, I got stung once and nearly died. It happened right after we were married. My throat swelled so tight I almost couldn't breathe."

"How did you get saved?" Rie asked, with eyes wide and frightened.

"Clarence drove me down to the drugstore and Mr. Welborn

gave me a shot of adrenalin. That's why I always carry this little vial of it in my pocketbook." And Momma opened her purse to show us the tiny bottle and a package with a syringe tucked inside.

"Oh!" That was all Rie said, but she sat very still, thinking about it for a while.

"Momma, why can't anyone but us wind honey on a spoon?" Rie was full of "whys" these days. "All the kids at school think it's funny 'cause I can wind honey and it doesn't drip. Why can't they do it too?"

"Well, maybe it's because their Daddies aren't beekeepers and didn't teach them how. Why can't you saddle a horse? Because. . ."

Rie interrupted, "Because I haven't *got* a horse, that's why!"

Well, that set us off laughing. We were still wiping our eyes when Daddy reappeared.

"Hey, come here and see what I found," shouted Daddy from the hillside. He stood beside the large trunk of an aspen tree that seemed to be scarred all over with black lines on its white bark. At first glance they all looked like claw scratches—from a bear perhaps. But no, a second look showed letters like "EDB" or "TH" and, around the other side, "R loves N" inside a crude heart. Some of them looked years old, with the black scar marks thick and swollen, while others seemed freshly done.

"Here's Momma's initials, right here," cried Rie. "Or maybe Aunt Edith's."

"Or Aunt Ethel's," chimed in Katy. "Can we do mine, Daddy?"

"Don't you think maybe that poor tree has enough scars already? Let's leave it in peace." Daddy started ambling back to the car.

"Please, Daddy," Katy said in her most wheedling voice.

"No honey bunch, we really shouldn't. Anyway, it's time to go or we won't get home when I promised."

As we left the picnic site, the road rapidly became a narrow trail with branches of oak brush scratching the sides of the Jitney and wildflowers growing between the tracks. We forded little streams, labored through mud holes, and finally came to a complete stop.

"We'd better not push our luck any further with this car. Let's hike on in," said Daddy. "Don't forget your sweaters; it's pretty chilly up here sometimes."

We were behind Saddle Mountain now, and everything looked different. New shapes, unknown peaks, snow lying in ravines far up the mountainsides—all a strange new world to me. The clouds, which had been little cotton balls at noon, were now becoming tall, dark thunderheads. The wind made the aspen leaves dance wildly and roared overhead through spruce trees. I was glad I wasn't alone up here, glad when we broke out into an open meadow bathed in sunlight.

"Oh my! Look at all the lupines. And the wild daisies. Oh, here's some columbine!" Momma exclaimed over each new discovery as if she'd never seen these things before. The columbine was especially pretty, I thought, shyly growing at the edge of the meadow under the shadow of the nearby trees. Its color was just right, its soft blue petals making a clear contrast against the shadowy green.

"We're about there now. Hear the creek down below in that draw?" Daddy pointed to the right, and as we followed him we could indeed hear the sound of water. Down the hill and into a ravine, along a narrow rocky trail we went. The creek was narrower and swifter here than at the picnic site.

"Here's the divider box," called Daddy up ahead. The man-made ditch left the creek at an angle, and the flow was controlled by a wooden damming device that could be moved up and down.

"Well, the divider is set right where I left it two weeks ago," said Daddy, "but there's not enough water going through. I wonder where the trouble is?" And he scratched his head thoughtfully. "Let's follow the creek up a little way."

Katy had already run ahead, surefooted as a mountain goat. "Daddy, Daddy," she called, "there's a dam up here."

"It's a beaver dam!" cried Momma. "Look at that."

"Well, I'll be darned. That's a big one, too," said Daddy.

It was a real engineering feat, all right, with logs six inches across and sticks and twigs, all carefully intertwined and caulked with mud and leaves. The beavers had built it so high that a part of the spillover went in a new direction, forming a small stream to one side.

"I'll have to get someone up here with me to blow that up," said Daddy, after reviewing the situation. "It's too big for me to do alone."

"Daddy! You're not going to blow up the beaver's home, are you?" Rie was indignant at the very idea.

An irrigation ditch with a divider box.

"I'll have to, I'm afraid, honey." You could tell Daddy didn't like the idea any better than Rie did. "Maybe I can leave part of it for them. We'll see."

The sun suddenly disappeared behind large blackening clouds, and the wind felt cold right through our sweaters. We started back to the car at a brisk pace—up the hill, through the meadow, and down the north slope. The Jitney was in sight as rain drops began to fall icy cold on our faces. And by the time we climbed into the car the rain was falling hard.

Daddy didn't even try to start the car but just sat there, seeming to enjoy the deluge. It left as quickly as it had come. The sun came out, making everything sparkling clean. The air smelled washed and new. I shivered a little as Daddy started the car and turned around to go down the narrow trail. And yet, by the time we had passed our picnic spot at the bridge and driven beyond the hay fields near Needle Rock, the air was warm again and the sun beat hot against the roof of the car. From April to July in thirty minutes!

16. Learning To Drive

THE JITNEY sat in Grandpa Drexel's driveway across the street freshly washed and ready to go one lovely fall Saturday morning. The Model A Ford had begun to show its age after twelve years of bumpy country roads, but Grandpa gave no sign of wanting to retire the family chariot. This was 1939, still a time of depression in Crawford, so he just polished and petted the old car and saved the money for more important things.

One of those more important things was piano lessons for his musical grandchild. We had recently found a good teacher who lived twenty-five miles away, west of Hotchkiss. Mrs. Lawlor had studied music in New York and planned a concert career until she fell in love with a western Colorado fruit rancher. For her, teaching a few students in the area was a way of using her talent. For me, it was a gift from God at a time when my training had come to a complete standstill. She was expensive enough, though—a dollar a lesson.

We went to lessons every Saturday morning. This meant a fifty-minute trip each way and an hour lesson. The only person who could take that much time away from work was Grandma. And so, all through my high-school years she drove me to my lessons. In fact, Grandma took four of her six grandchildren to Mrs. Lawlor for lessons for several years.

But today something more was going to happen. Today Grandma was going to start teaching me to drive. I ran across the street and waited impatiently by the car as Grandma hurried down the front steps with Grandpa right behind her. They looked like Mutt and Jeff when they stood together. I couldn't help laughing to myself.

"Well hello, Ol' Top" said Grandpa as he spotted me. "I hear you're ready to conquer the roads today." Half the fun of knowing Grandpa was hearing his newest pet names. He turned to Grandma. "Now Sis, you be careful. This Jitney's not so young anymore. Keep things under control—Please!"

"Oh Frank, everything's going to be fine. We'll be careful, won't we honey?" And she turned to me with a most reassuring smile.

"Nevertheless . . ." said Grandpa. But she wasn't listening. He left it at that and disappeared around the corner of the house.

This was a perfect late-fall day. The sun shone warm in a clear blue sky, bees and squirrels were busy gathering last-minute stores of food, and the birds sang carols of joy from fenceposts and telephone poles. New haystacks dotted the fields that were yellow with stubble or freshly plowed to await winter's snow. The roads had been freshly scraped and graveled in preparation for the bad weather ahead. Tumbleweeds bounced merrily along the fences, pushed by the passing breeze.

My heart pounded with excitement as I slipped into the driver's seat. Grandma showed me how to change the gears; how to put the clutch in and slowly, smoothly, let it out again; how to pull out the choke to start the engine and adjust it until the motor purred without a hiccup. When she did it, the operation seemed easy; when I tried it, everything jerked and sputtered. Grandma just laughed and kept me at it until, finally, we went rolling down the country road toward Hotchkiss.

"How can I tell where the wheels are?"

"See the radiator cap on the hood? Line that up on the right side where you want the wheel to go. It works perfectly." And sure enough, it did. So steering was easy.

My first real difficulty came about halfway up Rogers Mesa grade, a steep, narrow graveled road with sharp curves and no guardrails. By the time I had successfully negotiated the first turn, the engine began to struggle.

"Shift to second—fast!" cried Grandma. I did, but not fast enough. The engine sputtered again.

"Low!" she yelled. Too late—the engine coughed and died. Grandma grabbed the emergency brake and we just sat there trying to regain our composure.

As the weeks rolled by I learned how to change gears smoothly and could get to the top of Rogers Mesa grade without a single murmur from the engine as I shifted from gear to gear.

Then one day Grandma said, "Why don't you try to make it to the top in second gear?" Well! That would mean starting at the bottom at about thirty miles an hour and taking all those curves without braking or sliding at all. If I did it just right, and didn't meet anyone, I found I *could* get to the top in second. It became a weekly game and we'd laugh and shout and pound the steering wheel in delight whenever I was successful.

One driving lesson took place in the "dobies" north of Crawford. This area was once a vast grassland but was destroyed by greedy cattlemen in the late 1800s when they allowed their herds to overgraze there. Now the land is a barren waste of eroded clay soil that looks like a moonscape and is dotted with bone-white salt beds. Rattlesnakes, jackrabbits, and prairie dogs eke out an existence there along with smaller critters like lizards and mice. The casual observer would probably see no animal life at all, but if he were to stop and wait a few minutes, a prairie dog would suddenly pop out of a hole, sit on his haunches, and sniff the air in all directions.

"See that prairie-dog hole over there?" Grandma pointed to a mound about twenty feet off the road. "I want you to drive up to it and back the car all the way around it." Now *that* was an original idea if I'd ever heard one. We bounced off the road, the wheels of the car making perfect tracks in the fine dust of the adobe soil. However, Grandma wasn't satisfied with just going around the hole backwards—I had to inscribe a perfect circle in the gray dusty clay. It must have taken ten tries before she approved my effort, and even then she felt I needed more practice.

After that lesson I felt myself to be a quite proficient driver. But when I suggested that I was ready to try for a driver's license, Grandma shook her head and said that, no, there was a bit more to be mastered.

What, I wondered, didn't I know? I could handle all the worst curves, change gears, use the brake smoothly, drive backwards, and read all the dials. I even knew how to change a tire. My father had spent an hour helping me learn that dirty lesson. What was left?

The answer came unexpectedly. One day in late spring Grandma said, "Let's take the old road home from Hotchkiss today." I knew there was an earlier road south of the present graveled one, but I had never seen it. A warning thought flashed in my mind as I thought what this road might be like.

"Won't it be muddy Grandma?" I wondered. Only yesterday Grandpa had polished the car extra carefully, singing one of his favorite songs from *H.M.S. Pinafore* in a squeaky voice as he worked: "Oh he polished up the handle so carefully, that now he is the ruler of the Queen's Nav—vee."

It really wouldn't be nice to dirty up his clean car. He made another plea to Grandma just before we left that morning.

"Now listen here, ol' girl, try not to get into any trouble today. Sometimes you two take too many chances, you know."

"Yes, Dad, we'll be careful," Grandma had said cheerfully. But I noticed that Grandpa still looked unhappy as he waved us off.

In spite of my hesitancy, Grandma insisted that this was a perfect day to explore the old road. I suspected that she just relished adventure and wouldn't change her mind.

This road was indeed an old one—rutty, bumpy, hardly passable in places. I thought all my driving skills had been tested thoroughly when suddenly I jammed on the brakes in alarm. In front of me lay a narrow bridge with no rails. Worse, it was just two wide planks, one for each wheel. The approach down to it was muddy and steep and the other side looked just as bad. I couldn't go over that bridge! What if I slipped and we landed in the ditch below? My legs turned to jelly at the thought.

"Of course you can make it!" scoffed my intrepid instructor. "Just shift to low gear and keep your foot on the gas slow and steady. Never use your brakes, even if you slip a bit. You'll see, the car will go where you steer, if you keep the gas pressure steady. *No brakes, now!*"

My heart pounded wildly as we eased down the hill and on to the bridge planks. But the Jitney held stable and sure. Good old

My grandparents, Frank and Ella Drexel.

car! Then, just as we reached the far side I felt the rear wheels slip sideways. Almost by instinct I pushed the gas pedal to the floorboard. We shot forward off the bridge and careered crazily up the hill, slithering sideways as we went.

When we gained dry ground, I stopped and pulled the emergency brake. Grandma sat staring straight ahead, her hands gripping her pocketbook so tightly the knuckles showed white. Finally she smiled weakly and said in a small voice, "Whee! What a ride!"

As I looked at her I felt suddenly ten years older. The nerve of her! She was a daredevil! No wonder Grandpa always looked worried as he waved goodbye to us. He really was afraid for our safety, wasn't he! But I had to admit I had learned something about driving in mud. I would never be so afraid of it again.

Finally I found my voice. "Grandma, what can we tell Grandpa when he sees this muddy car?"

Grandma had regained her color finally. She turned to me, hesitated, then with a radiant smile she said, "Oh, we'll just tell him we took a shortcut home and ran into an unexpected mud puddle."

17. Reunion Time

SOMETIMES SUMMERTIME brought a very special event, when the whole Sipma family gathered to renew old ties. This happened whenever Gramma Den Beste's brothers and sisters could make the trip from Iowa with their families. Then the little log house, the bunkhouse, and the front and back yards would be filled with people—folks who could trace their beginnings to the Sipmas, who had come to the West from Iowa so long ago. There was Uncle Eddie, who had flaming red hair and dozens of funny stories. There was Uncle Stewart, who had no wife or children and wandered from job to job, mostly connected with the railroad. There was Uncle Garrit, who was quiet and unassuming. And, of course, Aunt Jennie and Uncle Ed Te Grotenhuis with their large family, plus all the Den Bestes with their children and grandchildren.

The reunion I remember best happened when I was about fifteen or so. Such excitement! Grampa had to borrow folding chairs from the church to accommodate the crowd. He set them in the front yard under the massive shade tree that Uncle Eddie had once dubbed "the million-dollar tree." Grampa also bought an extra barrel of water for the big event, and all the women prepared their very best Dutch dishes. By the time the crowd gathered during the morning of the big day, Gramma's dining table was filled to the edges with fried chicken, potato salad, roasting ears, green beans, peas, carrots, pies, cakes, cookies, and iced tea. On the back stoop some of the men stayed busy churning ice cream: a freezer of peach, one of strawberry, and one of plain vanilla.

There was much kissing and hugging and laughing and even crying, though most of the tears were the joyful kind. You could stand in one spot and feel an ocean of joy washing over everyone.

Finally, in the middle of all the hubbub, Grampa raised his hand and, when everybody had quieted down, he asked the blessing and led us in the Doxology. The rich sound of those dozens of voices raised in perfect harmony gave me goose pimples. It was better than the Mormon Tabernacle Choir! There was a moment of embarrassed silence, then the gradual murmur of voices began to grow again while we all lined up to fill our plates from the feast before us.

I had never thought much about all the dirty dishes that inevitably went along with such a meal until Leone, whom I now called "Aunt Leone" because of her marriage to Momma's brother Howard, suggested that it would be nice to let the women rest and visit while the young folks cleaned up. She organized about a dozen of us into an assembly-line crew. We formed one line from the table to the kitchen and another line back to the table again. Four unlucky kids drew the jobs of dish-scraper, dishwasher, rinser, and dryer. The rest of us passed the dishes along the line. Every few minutes we changed positions so no one would have the odious jobs for long.

The whole thing started as something of a chore, but soon it became a game. We had just started *tossing* the dishes along the line, when Gramma appeared in the doorway to see how things were coming along. For a moment she stood absolutely still, taking in the scene. Then, clapping her hands to her face, she uttered the only swear word I ever heard her use—a big, explosive "Haah," which rhymes with "hat" and translates roughly from the Dutch as "Damn!" In spite of her fears the whole job got done in record time and without a broken dish. We hung the wet flour-sack towels on the line out back, mopped the kitchen floor, took the food scraps out to the hog trough and, with a sense of real accomplishment, went to join the various games in progress.

There was softball in the old orchard, horseshoes behind the bunkhouse, storytelling under the shade tree, and anagrams in the living room. But the most exciting contest was in progress out on the croquet court.

Croquet was something of a passion with the Den Beste bunch. This was not the kind where you casually put down a few stakes and wickets and knock the balls around for a while—this was Croquet with a capital C. Grampa Den Beste had built his court just beyond the lawn on the flattest spot of clay he could find. He had leveled, measured, and rolled it to absolute perfection. Then he had set the wickets and stakes in exact positions and outlined the border of the court with lime dust.

A part of most summer Sunday afternoons at the Den Bestes had always been an ongoing croquet tournament. After dessert someone would say, "Okay, you guys, let's go! Who wants to start today?" There wasn't any formal organization about it, but during the course of the day anyone who felt brave enough would get a chance to take on the champions of the previous game while onlookers shouted encouragement and sideline strategies.

Daddy had built a court at our place, too. Since there was no level spot anywhere in the yard, he had constructed a rock wall near the top of the pasture and filled it in to make a level clay court. Like the one at the Den Bestes', it was a regulation-sized rolled-clay court, lined with lime. And it got used nearly every day all summer long. Momma and Daddy were too busy to play often, but Katy, Rie, and I spent hours and hours practicing and playing with one another.

A clay court takes constant maintenance: such things as watering down the dust, raking it smooth, pushing the heavy roller over the surface to pack it down, and brightening the border lines with new lime.

The rule at our house was: He who wants to play must fix the court himself. Since Katy was the most avid player, she did the job most of the time. Therefore, no one could be upset if she also became The Champ.

Katy was, in fact, hoping to become top player at the reunion and had practiced for days. She could take her ball more than halfway around the court in one turn and, given one extra ball to use, could play a whole game in one turn sometimes.

When we joined the spectators at the reunion tournament we found Katy, teamed with Grampa Den Beste, playing for all she

Seven of us enjoying watermelon during a July 4 get-together in about 1932. Watermelon was a rare treat.

was worth. They made a formidable pair. Uncle Roscoe (Aunt Edith's husband) and Uncle Raymond were their opponents and were very close to finishing the game when I arrived. Katy was a "rover," and Grampa had only the last two wickets to go through. This was going to be a close one!

On the sidelines we rooted for our favorites while the players battled for position and victory. Finally, Katy played a spectacular long shot across the court, hitting Grampa's ball, then used her ball to put him through the last wicket. His ball hit the stake as it rolled to a stop; Katy used her final shot to hit the stake with her ball and the cheers went up all around for little Katy and her Grampa. I'm sure there were more games that day, but that's the one I remember.

By evening, when the sun had disappeared in the west and left a blaze of orange sky behind, when everyone had talked, played, and eaten until appetites were sated and senses dulled, there was only one need left unfilled. We needed to sing. One hymn led to another. Then from hymns we changed to old familiar songs and tunes of long ago. The men teamed up in quartets. Aunt Kate and Uncle Bill sang their patter-song version of "Peggy O'Neil"—the one that goes:

Annie Rooney sets a fellow loony
And a million fellows get to feelin' spoony
When they meet Peggy O'Neil

Wilma Jean, the redheaded cousin, and Rie and I gave a rendition of "Home on the Range" and the lovely old hymn "Day is Dying in the West" in our own arrangements. The three of us had been singing trios together for over a year and had learned both special school-contest material and things we arranged ourselves. Then came "Red River Valley" and some spirituals. By the time the light had faded and left only stars and a full moon, we had sung ourselves into a stupor of contentment.

Families gathered empty dishes and sleepy children while the teenagers tried to wheedle from the grown-ups a little more time together. The big day had played itself out and now must be relegated to memory, where one could take it out occasionally, polish it off, and find the pearl of happiness still glowing softly.

18. Institute

GRANDMA DREXEL sat in one of the porch rockers, quite absorbed in the magazine on her lap, as I went up the steps with the afternoon mail.

"Here's a letter from Baltimore," I said as I handed her the envelope, then asked what she was reading. She showed me the page in *The Ladies Home Journal* called "If You Ask Me," a regular feature page of questions from readers and answers by Eleanor Roosevelt. Mrs. Roosevelt was a real heroine to Grandma. She was a woman who, in spite of physical limitations, was making herself known and admired all over the country. It didn't matter a whit that Eleanor was tall, awkward, plain, and the possessor of a thin and grating voice. Grandma saw all of her own defects in this famous woman and tried to learn from her. Mrs. Roosevelt's beliefs matched her own and seemed to strengthen her resolve to be a woman of consequence in her own small sphere.

"That's quite a bundle of mail you have there. I hope some of it is for you," said Grandma.

"Oh, it is!" She must have guessed my excitement. "It's the information sheet and schedule from Institute. Rie's going this year too. And our trio has been asked to sing at two of the programs."

"Institute time already? My, how fast the summer flies by!" It seemed to me to crawl sometimes, but the older folks *always* seemed to be saying "How time flies." Anyway, just a week from now we finally would make the exciting trip to the Institute grounds on Grand Mesa, where we would spend a glorious week with lots of other young people from the Methodist churches of western Colorado.

I'm not sure when Institute first started. The grounds were owned by the Methodist Church and used during July and August by various church groups and clubs such as 4-H, Campfire Girls, and so forth. When I was small the whole family went to Institute a time or two. Each church had its own cabin back then, and some of the families even pitched tents for the week's stay. The Crawford cabin was a good-sized one-room affair with a ladder to the floored loft above. The big fireplace at one end provided for heat, boiling water, and all the cooking. I remember very little of that experience except for being cold, feeling afraid up in the attic where all the women slept, and hating to walk out to the outhouse because it was muddy and mosquitoes buzzed furiously around me all the way.

Now there were two large dormitory cabins, one for girls and one for boys, an even larger building containing a kitchen and dining hall, a rustic but picturesque chapel, faculty cabins, a campfire circle, and a playground area for softball and badminton.

The camp was built along the southern edge of Baron Lake, one of the biggest and most accessible of Grand Mesa's many lakes. The north side of the lake was dotted with privately owned cabins and one or two tourist businesses, such as a boat house where rowboats could be rented by the day or the hour. Even though Grand Mesa was a bit hard to get to and its open season very short, it was a popular tourist area, with campgrounds, a hotel or two, and roads to several of the more spectacular lakes and lookouts. One of the scenic trips I remember taking with the family was on a corduroy road made of logs laid side by side where the land stayed spongy even in the summertime. This led to a lake full of water lilies; so full, in fact, that the mammoth pads and blossoms left little space for a sight of water. It would have been fun to be a frog in that lake. I wonder if a corduroy road is still there.

Our youth group met at the church with packed bags, bedrolls, and lots of citronella oil, without which no one should camp anywhere on Grand Mesa, even inside a cabin. There were about a dozen of us, plus a couple of adult chaperones and the driver of the truck who had volunteered to take us "up the hill."

The first half of the trip was a windy, dusty one as we rode down the country through Hotchkiss, over Rogers Mesa, and into the dry sage and salt lands beyond. But when we turned right at the cutoff to Grand Mesa everything began to change. It was all uphill, and the road passed through orchard country and the town of Cedaredge. Above that appeared scrub cedar and oak and, finally, an endless series of hairpin curves where the road became narrow and steep. The truck ground its gears as it labored up and up. The air turned cool, then chilly. The trees became increasingly taller and thicker, and beneath them lay a tangle of grasses and wildflowers. Look one way and you would see nothing but the mountain of trees; look the other and you saw mostly empty space, with a steeply sloping hill below. Then at last the truck topped the final ridge and a world of spruce, aspen, a sparkling lake, and a cobalt sky spread before us. We had arrived!

All the buildings were made of rugged logs with high steep roofs designed to withstand the great depth of winter's snow. There were paths through the trees from cabin to cabin and a large clearing between the cabins and the dining hall. A sizable campfire circle was laid out on one side of the clearing, near the girls' dorm. Between it and the lake stood a rough-hewn wooden cross. With the beauty all around, the strange and pungent odors of spruce, damp earth, and wood fires, and the air so thin and clear it made one's head swim, I already felt closer to God. At this ten-thousand-foot altitude we seemed to have climbed halfway to heaven.

And now we all struggled with our bags and bedding into the cabin where we slept. I hadn't expected luxury, but I'm not sure I was ready for such crudeness. In the girls' L-shaped building there were rows of double bunks made of rough boards and padded with straw mattresses. We kept our suitcases under the bunks and dressed wherever we could find room to stand. The building had electric lights and was tightly built and dry but there was no heat for the cold nights. We all snuggled into bed quickly at night! The bath house was primitive too. I don't recall much about it except that there was no hot water so we washed in record time. But then, this was *camp* after all, and it was all fun.

Each day went quickly, beginning with reveille and ending with taps and "lights out." In between the bugler's first and last calls we kept a busy pace: breakfast, morning chapel, classes; dinner, enforced rest, softball or hiking or boating; supper, evening chapel, campfire singing and prayer service; a few free minutes, bed. And yet there always seemed to be time to slip off alone for a bit of serious thinking. I sometimes sat on a rock that protruded from the southern slope of the hillside. From that vantage point I could see Cedaredge, Delta, Hotchkiss, and the mountains east of Crawford. And even beyond that, way off in the pale, blue distance were more mountain ranges—as far as the sight could penetrate were peaks and ridges, both east and south. How far away were they? A hundred miles? At least, I thought. It made one truly humble to think that in all that great and wonderful expanse of God's creation a tiny bit of humanity like me could matter to Him. But the Bible said it was so and I felt renewed and freshened every time I went to that place.

Our trio also took a few minutes each day to practice something for the evening's campfire service. The campsite circle, with the cross showing its silhouette between the fire and the water, was an inspiring place to perform. Nothing could be more moving than the experience of singing with others as the large bonfire sent sparks drifting heavenward, the wind played the lofty branches of the spruce trees like harp strings, and the night showed the immensity of space beyond, out there where the stars resided.

Rie and I had signed up to work in the dining hall to help pay our tuition for the week. It wasn't especially hard work—setting up tables, serving the meals, and clearing the tables afterward—but it did mean that we were usually one of the last stragglers on the path to the chapel in the evenings. Although most of the camp buildings were grouped around the open recreation area, the chapel was set off by itself east of the campus and deep in the trees. We always carried a flashlight with us to find our way to the evening program—except for one night we'll both remember forever.

We forgot the flashlight and, being late already, decided to try to make it through the woods by memory and moonlight. We had gotten no more than ten feet into the pathway when the moon disappeared. With the darkness came a roll of thunder and a warning flash of light. Talk about sudden! I'd never witnessed a thunderstorm moving so fast before. But there we were, in total darkness except for moments of flashing, with the storm coming closer and closer. We both shivered and stopped to decide what to do. Then it hit— how close neither of us could have said—but it hit so near that Rie was knocked to the ground and I felt my feet and legs tingle strangely.

Neither of us heard the other cry out, but in another instant we found ourselves clinging together unhurt. I remember nothing else about that evening. I can only assume we eventually found our way to the chapel and joined in with the rest of the evening's activities. The next day one of the older campers found what the lightning had *really* struck. It was a tree about fifty yards south of us and not far from the chapel. The tree was now a mass of ivory-colored splinters scattered all over the ground in every direction. It didn't seem to have been burned—it just exploded. It may be true that lightning never strikes in the same place twice, but it surely seems to dog some folks' footsteps. I wonder how many more times it will find me? And Rie?

Like all camp meetings, Institute had to end. Each year the last day came too soon. The truck from Crawford arrived to take us back down to the valley below, from our mountaintop experiences back to the realities of everyday life. It always meant tearful good-byes, promises to meet again next year, and many precious memories. But it also meant happy reunions with our families—none of us were usually gone from home so long. And one more thing: The new Montgomery Ward and Sears catalogues would have arrived while we were gone and would be there waiting for us. That treat came only twice a year in those days—an event we all eagerly awaited.

19. *The Double H Ranch*

THE BAY horse standing quietly in front of me looked huge. Was I really supposed to mount such an enormous beast all alone? How?

"Daisy is used to being mounted from the left side," Ned said, kindly enough, and with only a hint of condescension in his voice. "Stand here, take the reins in your right hand, and put your left foot in the stirrup. Then just grab the saddle horn with your left hand and throw your right leg over the horse." Ned was one year older than his sister Betty Jane, who had invited me to spend the weekend at their ranch. At sixteen, he seemed to me to be the most sophisticated and handsome young man I had ever met. But the truth was that I had never ridden a horse before, even though I had seen and lived near them all my life.

I put a timid foot in the stirrup, which dangled next to my waist. "Up and over!" said Ned, and Betty Jane gave me a gentle boost from the rear as I pulled my weight up over the waiting horse. Daisy didn't move an inch, but stood quiet and patient with her untrained rider. She had evidently put up with this experience many times before.

I felt better now that I was safely in the saddle and felt its smooth and comfortable shape. The world looked different from up here, too—wider horizons, more blue sky. The grasshoppers and weeds receded in importance while the trees seemed to gain in stature. I liked it!

Betty Jane showed me how to guide the horse by tightening the reins against the side of her neck.

"Don't worry about it, though," she said. "Daisy knows her way along all the paths and will follow my horse even if you forget to tell her."

Learning to handle the reins wasn't hard at all, but trying to keep my seat on a trotting horse *was*. We tried a canter, and that was much smoother. I wished we could canter all the way, but Betty Jane said the horses would soon tire at that speed on this rough range ground. Daisy seemed to like the trot better, and settled into it at every opportunity.

Out past the corral, down the lane, and into the nearest hay field we went. The mountains lay just behind us now, their familiar shapes completely changed from this angle. Down in Crawford the air was hot almost to burning on this August day, but up here at the higher elevation the breeze was brisk and cool. The sun burned, but did so unobtrusively.

I began to understand something of the size of this ranch as we rode past field after field of alfalfa, clover, and grain. The Double H Ranch, named for its cattle brand—two H's side by side—was known as one of the biggest and best in the whole area. The Allyns raised a large herd of cattle there, using the high hills for summer forage and raising all the winter feed in the lower fields. Their barn could be seen miles away with its white painted sides and the brand HH, painted in clear white lettering on the red roof.

Betty Jane slowed our horses to a walk as we entered a field of newly cut alfalfa where a crew of men was busily lifting bales of hay onto a wagon. Many ranchers still stacked their hay using a tall cranelike rig, called a Mormon Stacker, to lift bundles of loose hay to the top of a rapidly rising stack. But Ted Allyn had one of the new baling machines, which automatically bundled hay into tight rectangular bales and tied them with wire. After the bales had dried in the field for several days, they would be loaded on wagons and taken to the big barn or to smaller sheds in the fields.

"Where's that brother of yours?" asked one of the tired, dirty ranch hands as he spat a stream of tobacco juice on the ground.

"Don't get your dander up," said Betty Jane. "He helped saddle

A Mormon Stacker in use.

these horses for us and then had to go catch a pony for his little sister. He'll be up in a little while."

"Hope he brings some lemonade when he comes. That's what we sent him down for," scolded Mr. Allyn. Her father bossed the job personally, working just as hard as his crew did. He was a squat, solid man who had ridden so much during his lifetime that his legs were permanently bowed, making his walk look a little like a fat rooster's. His cowboy hat, worn at a rakish angle, shaded a handsome bronzed face with surprisingly delicate and artistic features. Ted Allyn was a complicated man who could outride anyone, yet he also played the piano and composed lovely songs in the swing style of the day. He spent many evenings playing and singing these songs or experimenting with a small electric organ.

"Let's go as far as the fishing pond, and then we'd better turn back," said Betty Jane as our horses meandered along the edge of another uncut field of alfalfa where a small empty shed awaited its bales of hay. I noticed a sudden gust of cold air and felt a slight chill as the sun disappeared behind a bank of dark, heavy clouds. They had certainly appeared suddenly, it seemed to me. The rapidly changing sky and the soreness beginning to invade the inside of my thighs made me more than willing to turn back any time Betty Jane was ready.

We had gotten to the pond, stopping to let the horses rest and munch a few tender stalks of clover, when the first rumble of thunder sounded in the southeast.

"Oh-oh," said B.J. "We'll have to hurry to beat the rain—come on!" And she started a brisk canter back toward home. I followed gladly, enjoying this easier gait, when suddenly a flash of lightning and an almost instantaneous clap of thunder exploded all around us. My gentle Daisy was not prepared for this. She suddenly became a wild thing, galloping across the field with one purpose in mind: to leave that frightening spot. I held on, my hands gripping the saddle horn and my knees hugging Daisy's flanks for all I was worth. I was too terrified to notice just how smooth this galloping stride felt. I only wondered if I could hold on, how I could possibly stop her, and what it might feel like to fall off.

My horse flew through the clover field, into the alfalfa field beyond it, and headed straight for the empty hay shed. I realized where we were going only in time to duck my head as we raced through the door. Daisy stopped as suddenly as she had started, nearly throwing me head over heels in front of her. The horse stood there trembling while I shivered and shook and realized I was still in the saddle with my arms grabbing Daisy's neck and the saddle horn cutting into my stomach.

By the time Betty Jane arrived I had straightened up a little and begun to wonder what to do next. Poor Betty Jane looked as white as a sheet, apparently afraid her friend was dead. I laughed weakly as she helped me down from the horse.

"How was that for a dude's first ride?" I asked, with a bit of pride showing in my voice.

"You did great—really!" That was high praise from someone so used to riding. Then she added, "But Daisy did a pretty good job of stopping without dumping you. Really, you should be grateful to her." I *was* grateful, also properly deflated.

We sat on the floor waiting for the rain to stop, not talking much, just watching the rain as it slowed to an occasional drip and enjoying the mixture of odors—warm damp horseflesh, the smell of freshly washed air, the sweetness of wet ripe alfalfa. When the sun reappeared, turning everything to a bright glitter, we remounted the now-quiet horses and started at a leisurely pace for home. We took a shorter route than on the way out, for which I was truly thankful. By now I felt sore all over and was ashamed to say so. This was all in a day's fun for Betty Jane, but for me it was like nothing I had experienced before. I looked at cowboys with a new sense of respect. How did they do this all day, every day?

The ranch house was a welcome sight. It nestled in a small valley in a most picturesque way: a large two-story rectangular structure, not imposing but certainly ample. Screened porches ran along the length of both floors of the west and south walls. Inside it was cool and inviting, with lovely parquet floors of solid wood, friendly over-stuffed sofas and chairs, and a long shining dining table where the large family and their frequent guests gathered.

I know now that the Allyns were wealthy, at least by Colorado mountaineer standards. But none of this was flaunted, and I was hardly aware of it then. Both Ned and Betty Jane went to Catholic schools in Denver and Boulder, not because of wealth but because the Allyn ranch lay outside Delta County. There was no way to get to their own county's high school because the Montrose County schools were all on the far side of the Black Canyon. Since geography forced them to go to a boarding school, their parents wisely decided to send them to the best ones available.

Betty Jane and I carried on a lively correspondence during the winter months, and we visited each other as often as possible during the summer, mostly at her place because there were so many ways there to occupy the time.

We spent this particular evening—Betty Jane, Ned, a cousin of theirs named Don, and I—playing cards out on the second-story porch and listening to the ranch hands making music under a tree near their bunkhouse. One fellow played a harmonica and another accompanied him on a guitar. It was relaxing, restful music—sad and happy all at the same time. I liked it as much as any music I've ever heard. When the music stopped we sat a little in silence, listening to crickets, frogs, and all the other night sounds of the country.

"Where do you think you'll be a year from now, Don?" asked Ned. "'Spose the war in Europe will be over by then?"

"I dunno," replied the older boy. "I kinda worry about it, you know. Seems to me Hitler has to be stopped before he gets any bigger ideas—like trying to conquer France, or something. I have a terrible feeling we'll have to go help England before it's all over."

"Would you join up if it came to that?" asked Betty Jane.

"Yeah, I guess so. Maybe I could become a flying ace." I could just see Don, splendid in an air force uniform.

But war was so far from this peaceful mountain valley that none of us could really imagine being involved in it. Sure, we heard the news on the radio. Everyone listened to Edward R. Murrow every evening. We knew that Hitler had just taken possession of Poland, that England had declared war on Germany, that Mussolini had become a dictator in Italy and had extended his hand into Africa, taking Ethiopia for his own. It seemed that all the headlines were about the war and all the newsreels at the Saturday-night movies showed nothing but marching armies. But that was a long, long way from Colorado and our happy existence there. We lived in a bubble that would soon enough burst and thrust us all into the realities of life. But in 1939 we were still safe and insulated, still living in prewar rural America, still having nothing better to do on a warm summer evening than sit on a ranch porch and play cards. And, for a greenhorn rider like me, nurse sore muscles and a raw bottom.

20. A Winter Weekend

THE WINTER of 1941 was a long and cold one. From the first snow-storm in early November it seemed evident that Dame Nature had set her mind on an "old-fashioned" winter. The mountains turned white from top to bottom almost immediately, and after three steady snowfalls during the middle of the month it was clear that we would see the ground no more until spring. Even a pleasant warm weekend for Thanksgiving didn't melt enough snow to clear the roads. What it did was turn the snow into slush, which froze into a permanent base for future storms.

For kids this was all good news. We could build a fort, stock-pile snowballs in it by the dozens, and play there day after day. The slide that the sixth-graders built on the slope between the upper- and lower-grades section of the schoolyard just stayed and stayed, getting slicker with each succeeding melt and freeze. The seventh-graders dug out a big circle in the snow with spokes radiating from the center like a wagon wheel for the usual game of fox-and-geese and used it for days with only the barest maintenance. And, of course, we could go coasting almost anywhere anytime we wanted to.

That's the way things were as we sat in the big study hall at school Friday afternoon and noticed yet another snowstorm begin-ning. Only the first week of December and already we could look out on this steadily falling curtain of white with as much annoyance

Needle Rock from one of the bee yards in winter.

as delight. More snow meant more paths to shovel, slower trips in the school buses for the country kids, more trouble with farm chores. It might be beautiful coming down, a picture of perfection as it piled high on tree branches and fenceposts, but it meant trouble, too, and no one could quite forget that.

By two o'clock Mr. Mulay had decided to close school early. If he waited until the usual four o'clock closing time the roads might be impassable out on the mesas.

The hallway filled with happy, shoving kids. Jackets, coats, overshoes, caps, and mittens seemed to fly in all directions as everyone tried to be first in line for the buses.

For the hundredth time I said a little prayer of thanks for being lucky enough to live in town and thus able to walk home. For me this snow would be pure pleasure. I didn't have to shovel paths or break ground out to the barn or haul wood or get the cows in from the far field. I could leisurely walk along watching snowflakes fall on my arms and marveling at their infinite number of patterns. I could scoop up a handful and eat it, cold and pure and tasteless. And I could stand still and enjoy the fairyland that was being created before my eyes as fences became patches of white filigree and trees turned into statues of abstract beauty.

When I got home, Rie and Katy were already there and Momma

was busy taking fresh bread out of the oven. Can there be a more delicious aroma than freshly baked bread, just sliced and waiting for cold sweet butter to melt on it? Add a trickle of honey and you have one of life's rare treats.

I had just finished the last bite of bread when Daddy came in with two buckets of coal.

"Try not to bring in snow on your boots, Clarence," warned Momma. "How much more work yet? Can't you quit soon?"

" 'Fraid I'll be kinda late before it's all done," Daddy replied in a surprisingly weary voice. "Haven't gotten in the kindling yet or milked Suzy. She'll have to have extra feed handy, too. And then I've got to go replace two burned-out street lights at the other end of town and check in on Dad across the street to see if they need anything."

Suddenly I felt terribly selfish. To think that I had assumed I needn't do any chores! Now it seemed pretty obvious that there was work waiting for all of us.

"I'll get the kindling, Daddy," I said, "and I can check at Grandpa's too. Katy, why don't you help Daddy get the hay down for Suzy? Rie is going to help Momma with supper."

I wrapped up again, buckled up my overshoes, and went out to the wood house. The box on the back porch was nearly empty, so it took four trips to get it filled to the top and to load the box behind the kitchen stove. When I got to Grandpa's house the walks and steps were completely covered under this new blanket of snow. I didn't even need to ask what must be done—it was obvious that a path would have to be shoveled down to the street and another to the cellar. Grandma was already out working, so I joined her in the task. It was heavy wet snow and I tired quickly, but Grandma seemed to be made of iron. She shoveled away steadily, stopping only to admire the beauty all around us and to listen to the peculiar silence that engulfs a world in the midst of a snowstorm.

Saturday dawned cold and still and brittle. The only heat in my upstairs bedroom came from a ventilator cut into the ceiling of the living room below. I stuck my hand out from under the bed covers and felt for the reassuring bit of warm air rising through the vent. I had learned to put on most of my clothes while I was still under the covers, then to hop right out over the vent, where

I could hastily pull on the last layer. Then I made a mad dash for downstairs and *warmth*.

Daddy already had news that the county road-graders weren't going to be able to make it to Crawford at least until tomorrow, so roads in general would be dangerous. That meant no trip to Mrs. Lawlor's for a piano lesson. Grandma would have taken on the challenge anyway, but Grandpa put his foot down and said flatly, "No."

The day went fast, even without the trip. My Saturday chores included dusting the floors and furniture all over the house, studying the Sunday school lesson, picking out music for next day's church service, and practicing at least two hours. Since I wouldn't have a lesson, I'd just practice longer.

When Daddy came in at dinnertime he had more news: A big coasting party was being planned for this evening. Somebody in town had gotten permission to officially close the main road through town after 6:00 P.M., so we could set up a coasting track all the way from the telephone office at the top of the hill down to the bridge at the bottom of the canyon. What a run! It included two ninety-degree turns and a final sharp curve right at the bridge.

The news spread fast, and by nightfall people began to gather from all over town. Some of the young men gathered enough firewood for a bonfire and built it near the top of the hill. Marshmallows appeared as if by magic, and a couple of big logs to one side of the fire provided a resting spot.

"Wanna ride down the hill with me?" asked Gilbert shyly at my side. "This sled's old but it goes good." Gilbert was a year older than I—tall, awkward, homely, nice.

Rie and Katy had already taken off on our sled, so I said, "Sure."

"I'll steer and you push. Okay?" And off we went. The snow was wet and packed, the sled runners slick as glass, the course steep. Here came the big curve! Drag one foot—lean hard to the left—pull on the steering bar. And around the bend we sailed with just inches to spare. Now the bridge seemed to fly toward us—and suddenly someone in front of us took a spill. We veered off to one side to avoid hitting them and smashed into a snowbank: snow in the eyes, the mouth, the nose—what a ride!

By the time we had dusted all the snow off and checked for

broken bones, other couples had joined us at the bottom of the hill. We all started the long cold hike up the hill together.

And then the best part of the whole party happened. Mr. Porter, who ranched just a mile or so down the canyon, appeared on the scene with a team of horses and a tow line.

"Hop on your sleds, kids, and grab the tow line. Ol' Dan and Tuck here'll give you a lift up the hill." And that's just what Ol' Dan and Tuck did—over and over. Of course, we fed them marsh-mallows as payment.

The party ended when the last stick of wood had been thrown on the bonfire. It was just too cold to stay out long without a place to warm up now and then.

As I climbed the stairs to my room that night I heard something that made me stop dead in my tracks. What was it: dogs barking or mountain lions howling? Was it one voice or ten? Daddy must have heard it too because he came out to the back porch where I stood on the stair landing and listened with me.

"Don't hear coyotes much anymore," he mused softly. "But back when I was a kid they had songfests like that nearly every night. I always figured they were howling just for the fun of it. They've learned to keep quiet these days, now that they've been hunted almost to death. I sorta miss 'em." The eerie concert didn't last very long but I was glad I'd heard it, and when all was still again I "sorta missed 'em" too.

The next day should have been a very quiet one. After all, nobody could go anyplace until the graders got through to clear the roads. After an unusually small Sunday school and church gathering and a very quiet Sunday dinner, Momma settled down for a nap. Daddy worked on some accounts at the desk, and the rest of us found books or games to occupy our time.

And then the phone rang. It was Uncle Frank and he sounded really agitated.

"Have you heard? It's on the radio—Pearl Harbor has been bombed by the Japanese! You'd better turn on your radio and hear what's going on."

I was so shocked I didn't even quite know what he had said. The best I could do was to tell Daddy to "turn on the radio, please— it's awful—Hawaii is being bombed or something."

The Drexel sisters in December 1938. From left: *Katy, Rie, and me.*

The rest of the day was a blur, with everyone in town calling one another to repeat and embellish the news. Ears stayed glued to radios all afternoon and evening as newscasters tried to make sense of what was happening and what it could mean.

Monday morning the talk at school was on one subject only: What would happen now? Would the U.S. go to war? At ten o'clock that morning Mr. Mulay went around to all the schoolrooms and told us to gather in the study hall right away. He brought in a radio and we listened together as President Roosevelt addressed Congress with those historic words: "Yesterday, December 7, 1941—a date which will live in infamy," and went on to ask Congress to declare war against Japan.

It had come at last. No longer could we continue to enjoy our quiet, happy lives here in these hills, unmoved by the upheaval happening everywhere in the world. Perhaps last night the coyotes had sensed the coming events as they sang their mournful concert in the night.

21. Leaving

NINE OF us graduated from Crawford High School in the spring of 1943. We had started first grade together in 1930 in the same building where we now planned our final flings: Kid Day, Prom, and the graduation ceremony. Now we must say goodbye to security and enter the real world. There had been more of us back in those early grades, but through the years some moved away, some stopped school to go to work, and when the war started, one left high school to join the navy. Of the nine, only three were boys. Oscar and Dorrel would probably be in the military soon enough. Earl had been accepted at Denver University and was exempt from service because he planned a career in the ministry. I was the only girl who planned to go to college. The others had various plans for jobs, helping at home, marriage, business or beauty school.

It seemed to me that I had always planned to go to college to study music. It had never entered my head to do anything else. I applied to the university at Boulder because it offered the best scholarship program, and I was thrilled when I was accepted.

However, as those last summer days at home raced past, I found myself strangely divided—of two minds at once. How could I ever leave this place? How could I say goodbye to my family and all the people I cared for? Where could I turn for advice, friendship, help? Each time I thought about it my heart raced in panic. And yet,

The Drexel sisters in 1943. From left: *Myrtle, Rie, Katy.*

on the other hand, many a cool evening I sat on the porch looking off to the east where Saddle Mountain and the Castle Range lay in silvery, dark blue silence, drenched in moonlight and mystery. What was it like beyond them? They were a wall between me and life—between me and my future. I could hardly wait to begin the adventures that would open before me on the other side.

Fortunately, there weren't many hours left for exciting or frightening thoughts. I needed clothes, which I would have to make myself. I needed to practice enough to please the college professor who had offered me free lessons as a special scholarship. But most of all, I needed to earn money. I worked when and where I could: ironing for one woman, cleaning for another, helping in the kitchen of a ranch family during their haying season. That was hard work, but it paid well—a dollar a day plus room and board. In three weeks I earned the grand sum of twenty-one dollars.

All too soon it was time to sort my possessions, pack the trunk, and say goodbye. Leaving day was painful. There was room only for Momma, Daddy, me, and the trunk in the Jitney, so I had to say goodbye to Rie, Katy, and the grandparents in Crawford. I've tried several times to remember what we said to one another in farewell, but my mind has blocked it all out—except for one last moment when Grandpa waved and smiled as he said, "Tell the college president 'hello' for me." And so I laughed instead of cried as I waved goodbye. And then we were off to Delta to meet the train.

We stood, the three of us, beside the track when the train huffed and puffed into view and then slowed to a stop, spilling steam from its big noisy engine. I seemed to be in a trance then as I climbed the steps of the train, saw my trunk being rolled away to the baggage car, and watched Momma and Daddy waving to me—waving, and waving, and waving . . . .

The other side of the mountains did open a new world of knowledge and opportunities. I absorbed all I could during that time at school. But more importantly, I met the man of my future. Tall, dark, handsome, and still dressed in uniform, Louis had just returned from three and a half years in the army, doing his bit to win the war. Along with many, many other veterans, he hoped to use the money offered by the new G.I. Bill to finish his education and planned to enter a university in North Carolina.

Everyone in the family liked Louis very much, but the idea of my moving clear across the United States was quite a shock. Daddy and Grandpa Drexel seemed to think it was a fine idea, and Grandma clearly wished she could go, too. But Momma was tearful at the very thought. So far away! When would we come back? When could she visit us?

It *was* far away in those days, by train or car nearly a week of steady riding. Air travel was in its infancy and almost nonexistent for us. We could talk by phone, of course—that is, if the occasion was important enough for someone to walk up to the drugstore, place the call, and wait for the person at the other end to return it. Long-distance phoning was used mostly for dire emergencies or messages of great importance.

So once again I faced the prospect of leaving home. And once more I was conscious of both excitement and fear. However, we had only a month to prepare for the wedding. Momma had already made my wedding dress and needed only to make last-minute adjustments. Rie and Katy would be my bridesmaids and would wear the prom dresses they already owned.

Mrs. Lawlor, my old piano teacher, seemed pleased to be asked to play for the wedding, and Mary Edith agreed to sing. Earl became

Louis's best man. Ralph was asked to usher along with Rie's very special boyfriend, George.

Betty Jane's mother hosted a lovely shower. Aunt Kate arranged with neighbors to decorate the church with cut flowers. Grandma and Aunt Grace became hostesses to the out-of-town guests. Gramma Den Beste helped prepare all the goodies for the reception at our house after the ceremony. And Louis asked his cousin, who also happened to be my minister at the university, to officiate.

But what should we do about a possible shivaree? Newlyweds in the frontier days of the West were traditionally treated to a "shivaree," an old custom of uncertain origin involving a serenade accompanied by noisemakers such as pots and pans. This was followed by a party, gifts of food, and usually a bit of rowdiness. All this would take place a day or two after the wedding and at the home of the new couple.

In the beginning I suppose shivarees were just a spirited housewarming. But on the frontier they often involved boisterous and even cruel jokes. Daddy told us that at the conclusion of his and Momma's own party a group of fellows took him to town and made him walk home, a number of miles, while Momma sat at The Ranch, where they lived at first, and cried.

Another story, which was told as absolute fact, was that one new groom was taken from the wedding party by his buddies and locked up in the Crawford jail all night while his bride was left locked in their bedroom until both were released the next day. The picture is clearer when you know that the Crawford jail was just a dirt cellar dug into the hillside west of the church. It had a thick plank door, a small barred window, a straw mattress on an iron cot, a slop jar, and no heat. I don't suppose it's even there anymore.

By the time of my wedding, most couples didn't go to new homes in the same community, and shivarees evolved into just fun and stunts right after the ceremony and reception. Occasionally a few of the old ways persisted, holding up some couples for several hours while a bit of foolishness could be accomplished.

And so I worried a little about my fun-loving relatives. Although they knew we had a close schedule to keep, I felt sure they would try to do something to the car to give us a bit of discomfort.

So Louis and Daddy put their heads together and devised a plan.

First they visited an old retired rancher who lived just up the hill from us and who had a dilapidated, unused garage near the house. He happily agreed to let us hide our car there, and Daddy carried our suitcases up to the car early in the morning. Our plan was to leave the house after the reception and jump into the Jitney, where Daddy would be waiting and ready to take us up the hill in a hurry to our hidden car.

All went well—the wedding, the reception, and even the getaway—at least for a little while. But Earl, Ralph, Lester, Raymond, and Howard all piled into their cars when they saw what was happening. I told Louis to go east toward the mountains rather than west through town, thinking to outwit the fellows. (I knew a roundabout way to get back down from the hills without going through Crawford.) But the pursuers saw our dust and followed fast.

We seemed to be winning the race when I saw something just ahead that only a cruel fate could have supplied. A herd of sheep—a very *large* herd of white, woolly critters—filled the road ahead from fence to fence. If they had been coming toward us it might have been possible to find a path through them in time to get away. But the sheep were headed for the hills, and so we could proceed only inch by inch. In no time at all our tormentors had pulled up to the sheep and were out of their cars and pushing through the herd to our car. We rolled up the windows, locked the doors, and resigned ourselves to our fate.

I must admit, though, that my relatives were quite gentle with us. They painted every inch of our car with garish and indecent signs, tied cans to the bumpers, and escorted us back through town at five miles per hour with gleeful shouts and singing. Louis was properly embarrassed, but I felt mostly gratitude for having been dealt with so kindly.

Three years later, when Rie and George planned their wedding, they remembered our experience and decided on quite a different plan. They arranged to spend their first night in Grandma and Grandpa Drexel's upstairs bedroom, but they left their car at our gateway in plain sight and obviously packed for travel.

Toward the end of the reception Rie went to the upstairs bedroom to change from her wedding gown while George quietly disappeared to the foot of the stairs on the back porch. They had a close call when one guest spotted George, but the man must not have told on them because they managed to slip out the back way and go "down cellar" to hide. They chose a dark corner behind some shelves full of canned corn and beans and had a grand time listening to the frustrated crowd above as it searched indoors and out for its prey.

After waiting for the last guest to leave, Rie and George simply walked across the street to Grandma's, still undiscovered.

I have wondered often in recent years if the original shivaree has by now completely disappeared from the culture of the Southwest, as has so much else. The Old West of cowboys and Indians, of gold strikes and free land is gone, of course. But the beauty of the mountains, the strange allure of the dry but colorful desert, the glorious song of the meadowlark, and the soothing music of a mountain stream—all are still there.

Although I live in North Carolina, every now and then those mountains and canyons call to me and I pack my bag and head Out West again.

Epilogue

MY TEN-DAY vacation has nearly ended. I have visited many people and places, renewed old ties, and remembered things past. But one thing remains undone: I haven't yet visited Muggsie's grave in Grandpa Drexel's backyard. I hope I can still find it and its small headstone after all these years.

Muggsie remained a part of the family and a special friend to Grandpa in his last years, after Grandma died. When Momma and Daddy moved across the street to care for him, Muggsie went right along. She was getting pretty old by then and stayed increasingly close to Grandpa.

She certainly had all the comforts any cat could want. As she lost her teeth Grandpa began to oversee her diet. And when her legs stiffened with arthritis he built a special box for her on the enclosed back porch.

The box was snug with a carpet of old blanket cloth. It was elevated about a foot off the floor, and a ramp led from its door to a cat door in the outside wall of the porch. In the winter Grandpa installed a light bulb in the box for added warmth.

Muggsie didn't live as long as Grandpa, who made it to the grand old age of ninety. But she was beginning to show white hairs when she finally died at nineteen. Daddy dug a grave in the middle of a bed of delphiniums and Shasta daisies, near one of the spruce trees in the backyard. Then Grandpa went to work in his cellar workshop.

Muggsie, the family friend, in her old age.

The backyard of the Frank Drexel home. Grandpa is at the root-cellar door.

He made a tiny marble headstone and engraved a legend on its surface.

Thinking about all this, I walk up the driveway from the street to the backyard and spot the flower bed. There aren't any flowers, of course, but the spruce tree is there, towering a good thirty feet above me. And yes! There it is. The little marble marker leans to one side and is somewhat buried in the deep, fragrant spruce needles. But stooping down, I can still make out the words so carefully engraved:

GOOD FRIENDS
Tip your hat!
Here lies Muggsie,
Our late lamented cat.
In life she was
And once more may be
A DAISY
—1955—